"The distinctive contribution of *The Magnificent Story* is its attentiveness to the power of stories to destroy us, diminish us, and deprive us, or to free us, redeem us, and empower us. Spiritual formation teachers have occasionally known the power of story, but none has it so central as James Bryan Smith. I consider *The Magnificent Story* to be a long leap into the deep graces of spiritual formation, not just for individuals but for small groups and churches."

Scot McKnight, Julius R. Mantey Professor of New Testament, Northern Seminary

"'We are story-making people,' James Bryan Smith writes. But what if the stories we tell and live are too small? What if the gospel story is truer, better, and more beautiful than we have ever imagined? As only a seasoned minister could, Smith asks and answers these questions with practicality and passion, theological lucidity and love. As he so importantly captures in these pages, the story of Jesus doesn't just prepare us for the moment of death, but for every breathing, pulsing minute of life."

Jen Pollock Michel, author of *Teach Us to Want* and *Keeping Place*

"The gospel is declared to be good news, but sometimes the way we hear about it sounds more like potentially good, technically good, or 'someday' good news—like a life insurance policy. *The Magnificent Story* helps us see and feel the goodness, beauty, and truth of that good news right here and right now. What a welcome kingdom gift to the people of God! I'm so grateful for this inspiring and energizing vision of the gospel."

Alan Fadling, president and founder of Unhurried Living, author of *An Unhurried Leader*

"If Dostoevsky is right in making the observation that 'beauty will save the world,' then James Bryan Smith has provided us with an exquisite exposition of what this means and how beauty is revealed in the God story. And he does so without in any way downplaying the deep fragmentation of our world; to the contrary, Smith demonstrates that it is precisely against the backdrop of this deep pain that we see and know the beauty of God and thus the salvation of God."

Gordon T. Smith, president, Ambrose University, Calgary, Alberta, author of *Called to Be Saints*

T0318084

"Our current obsession with entertainment indicates, I believe, that we are starved for beauty. We long to be truly astounded. James Smith leads us in immersing ourselves in beauty that is drenched in goodness and truth, bringing abundant life."

Jan Johnson, author of *Meeting God in Scripture* and *Abundant Simplicity*

"Currently, James Bryan Smith is the best author I know for blending essential spiritual insight with fruitful spiritual practices. In *The Magnificent Story*, Jim is characteristic: by giving us spiritual practices that help us abandon our shriveled life stories, he helps us to sync our lives up to the good, beautiful, and true story of God—and become human as God intended."

Todd Hunter, Anglican bishop, Churches for the Sake of Others

"What story do you believe you are living in? No question is more important—or more frequently ignored, to the detriment of humanity. The vast totality of our afflictions—in the face of our deepest longings— is in no small part a reflection of the stories in which we believe we live, witting or not: stories that are the antitheses of goodness, beauty, and truth. But thanks be to God, with *The Magnificent Story*, James Bryan Smith has drawn back the curtain on the real cosmic drama in which we find ourselves. And if ever the plots of the stories of our lives have needed this book, that time is now. If you hunger for goodness, beauty, and truth, and moreover, if they have felt out of your story's reach, do not despair. For within these pages lies the chronicle your life has been waiting to read, to hear, to live."

Curt Thompson, author of *Anatomy of the Soul* and *The Soul of Shame*

"In *The Magnificent Story*, James Bryan Smith invites us out of the shrunken stories of a fear-based and formulaic gospel into a genuine encounter with the exquisite beauty of Christ. Smith points us to the practices of 'soul training' by which our lives can be formed in beauty, goodness, and truth. A most welcome and helpful book!"

Brian Zahnd, pastor of Word of Life Church, St. Joseph, Missouri, author of *Beauty Will Save the World*

THE
Magnificent
STORY

Uncovering a Gospel of
Beauty, Goodness & Truth

JAMES BRYAN SMITH

An imprint of InterVarsity Press
Downers Grove, Illinois

InterVarsity Press
P.O. Box 1400, Downers Grove, IL 60515-1426
ivpress.com
email@ivpress.com

InterVarsity Press® is the book-publishing division of InterVarsity Christian Fellowship/USA®, a movement of students and faculty active on campus at hundreds of universities, colleges, and schools of nursing in the United States of America, and a member movement of the International Fellowship of Evangelical Students. For information about local and regional activities, visit intervarsity.org.

Cover design: Cindy Kiple
Interior design: Jeanna Wiggins
Cover image: Moonlight Birds by Al-Attar, Suad / Private Collection / Bridgeman Images

Photo on page 15: photo by Mikhail Evstafiev. Wikimedia Commons.
Anastasis icon on page 118: Descent into Hell, icon from the Ferapontov Monastery, Moscow school, Dionysius and his workshop. Wikimedia Commons.
The song on page 93 is "Labor of Love" by Andrew Peterson. Used by permission of the author.

ISBN 978-0-8308-4637-5 (paperback)
ISBN 978-0-8308-4636-8 (hardcover)
ISBN 978-0-8308-8928-0 (digital)

Printed in the United States of America ∞

Library of Congress Cataloging-in-Publication Data
A catalog record for this book is available from the Library of Congress.

P 21 20 19 18 17 16 15 14 13 12 11 10 9 8 7 6 5 4 3 2 1

Y 35 34 33 32 31 30 29 28 27 26 25 24 23 22 21 20 19 18 17

To my daughter Hope

who inspires me with how much she loves living

in the magnificent story.

CONTENTS

How to Get the Most Out of This Book

THIS BOOK IS INTENDED TO BE USED in the context of a community—a small group, a Sunday school class, or a few friends gathered in a home or coffee shop. Working through this book with others greatly magnifies the impact. If you go through this on your own, only the first four of the following suggestions will apply to you. No matter how you use it, I am confident that God can and will accomplish a good work in you.

1. *Prepare*: Find a notebook or journal with blank pages. You will use this journal to answer questions sprinkled throughout each chapter (in boxes) and for the reflection on the soul training exercises (instructions are at the end of each chapter).

2. *Read*: Read each chapter thoroughly. Try not to read hurriedly, and avoid reading the chapter at the last minute. Start reading early enough in the week so you have time to digest the material and to do the exercise.

3. *Do*: Complete the weekly Soul Training Exercise. Engaging in exercises related to the content of the chapter will help deepen the ideas and narratives you will be learning. It can

also be healing, as it connects you to God. The exercises in this book are best done over several days.

4. *Reflect*: Make time to complete your written reflections. You may not be a journaling type, but I encourage you to find some way to keep track of your answers to the box questions as well as your reflections on the exercise.

5. *Interact*: Come to the group prepared to listen and share. If everyone takes time to write out answers in advance, the group conversation will be much richer, and your time together will be more effective. Remember the group discussion rule: listen twice as much as you speak. But do speak! The other group members will learn from your ideas and experiences.

6. *Encourage*: Interact with each other outside of group time. Use technology to stay in touch with the members of your group between gatherings. One good idea is to have a group email thread in which someone posts a thought or idea or question, and others can chime in. Another great thing to do is intentionally email at least one person in your group each week with an encouraging word.

LONGING FOR A MAGNIFICENT STORY

What kind of life does the Christian story give rise to?
This question is important, since the answer to it
determines the shape of our spirituality.

SIMON CHAN

WHEN MY DAUGHTER HOPE WAS LITTLE, I told her a bedtime story every night. I read her the usual books—*Goodnight Moon* and *Winnie-the-Pooh*—but her favorite stories were the "made-up ones." The made-up ones started when we were a bit rushed, having gotten in late, and I wanted to turn the lights out so she could get a full night's sleep. This was a bit of lazy parenting on my part. She asked for a book, but I said, "No, it's late, and time for lights out."

"But I want a story, Daddy," Hope pleaded.

"Okay, I will tell you a story," I said. So I thought about it and got an idea. I would tell a story in which *she would be the main character.*

"Once upon a time," I began, "there was a giant who lived all alone in a beanstalk in the sky. He had a goose who could lay golden eggs. Then one day a little girl named Hope ..." She let out a subtle gasp. She was not expecting it. I looked at her and she looked at me, and she smiled. I went on to tell the rest of the story, all the way up to the "The End." It was time to pray and go to sleep, but she was not ready. She was full of energy. My parenting trick had backfired.

"Tell it again, Daddy, please tell it again."

Years later, when she was a teenager, Hope told me those were her favorite bedtime stories. I reflected on why and have concluded she loved those best because *she was in the story*, not just witnessing it. I think it is the clue to understanding how we are designed. We were made not just to enjoy stories but to enter them. We long to take our lives, our stories, and merge them with another story. This is truly what we long for. But we desire more than a children's bedtime story. We were made for something much bigger.

WHAT'S YOUR STORY?

"What's your story?"

That is a common question we ask when we are getting to know someone. We are asking things like, "Where are you from? Are you married? What do you do for a living?" Once we gather this information, we come to know their story. But I ask this question with a different intent. When I ask to know someone's story, I want to know what story they are living by. What story is shaping their life?

We are story-making people. We love stories (Once upon a time ...). Our narratives help us make sense of our world. The big questions in life are, What is God like? Who am I? What is the meaning of life? What can I count on? What is the good life? What are my deepest needs? When we put together our answers we have a *metanarrative*, a large story that is capable of answering life's key questions. This story operates at a higher level, and once it is adopted it becomes a part of our unconscious mind. We do not have to think about the story consciously. We realize it's there only when it has been threatened.

Our stories are running our lives—in ways we may not even be aware of. Let's say your family led you to believe you are inadequate. They communicated this to you in many ways, usually not through words. Perhaps it was a disappointed glance or a failure to listen to you. The story of your inadequacy becomes a defining narrative of your identity, and it will shape your decisions and actions and feelings for many, many years. It does not matter whether the narrative is true or not. All that matters is that you believe it to be true.

What story have you been told about God? What have you been told about the gospel or about the Christian life, about Jesus, about the cross, about who you are, or about heaven? Your answers to these questions form a story that will determine how your life will go. If you wrote down your answers to these questions—if you told me the story you have been told, the stories you are telling yourself— and sent them to me to read, I believe I could predict how your life is going and will go *without having met you.*

The answers would reveal your ability to trust, to love, and to hope. I would know your capacity for courage. I would even be able to determine your level of joy—because the stories you are living by are running your life. You are living at their mercy.

If what I am stating is true, then the most important thing we can do is to start living into the right story. Any story worth giving the power to shape our lives must pass a simple test: Is it beautiful, good, and true? If it is, then it is a *magnificent story.* You were designed for nothing less.

THE MAGNIFYING POWER OF BEAUTY,
GOODNESS, AND TRUTH

The word *magnificent* is defined as that which is beautiful, good, and true. The root word is *magnify*, which means to enlarge, enhance, and expand. When something is magnificent it has the power to magnify. That is what Mary said to her relative Elizabeth in her famous speech we call "the Magnificat": "My soul magnifies the Lord" (Luke 1:46). Mary had just learned the amazing news that she would bear a Son who would save the world. This good news led her—in the depths of her soul—to magnify the Lord. The story of the annunciation is an example of beauty, goodness, and truth.

Here is the story in a contemporary form: "Catch this: God is going to become human. God has chosen a lovely young woman of deep faith to conceive and bear and raise this child, who is fully God and fully human. Wow. And she is going to agree—to say, 'Let it be unto me.' She will suffer, but every generation will call her blessed. God is going to move into our neighborhood and pitch his tent among us in order to save us." The story of Advent, the Christmas story, is beautiful and good and true.

What makes something beautiful, good, or true? Beauty, goodness, and truth are called the three *transcendentals*. This is because they transcend—or stand above—the physical realm. They are real, perhaps more real than the physical realm. They are invincible and unbreakable, too powerful to be changed. The Greek philosopher Plato was the first person to link them together and speak of them as a group. Plato was interested in the purification of our souls, and he believed that the three transcendentals could ennoble the soul. In this book you will encounter the word *transcendental* many times.

BEAUTY

Thomas Aquinas said beauty is "that which, when seen, pleases." Beauty is the combination of several elements that, when put into the right form, are pleasing. On the campus where I teach there are rosebushes. When they are in bloom, I love to stop and—well, you know—smell the roses.

What makes something beautiful? Theologians such as Augustine of Hippo, in the fourth century, and Aquinas, in the thirteenth century, wrote about the components of beauty, such as clarity, proportion, wholeness, and harmony. Most people see a rose and find it to be beautiful. The color, shape, and texture of the rose are what we see, but their combination is what makes it beautiful.

We do not need to understand the qualities of beauty to know it or to love it. The slogan in an ad for a luxury car reads, "Performance that moves you. Beauty that stops you in your tracks." Even though it is an advertising slogan, it tells an important truth: beauty is very powerful. It really does *stop us in our tracks*. Many people who gaze on the Grand Canyon find themselves at a loss for words. Most people are affected by the beauty of a car, a home, a flower, or a sunset even if they are not conscious of it. There are higher and deeper objects of beauty that may be more difficult—perhaps even impossible—to see.

Music, architecture, poetry, pottery, photography, food preparation and presentation, painting, carpentry, and interior design are evaluated by our sense of beauty. I enjoy watching home renovation television shows. At the end of the show (the big reveal), as the people walk through their newly renovated and redecorated homes, they all say the same thing: "Wow, it is so beautiful!" I once counted the number of times people in the show used the word *beautiful*: eleven times in two minutes.

I went with my wife, Meghan, to St. Martin's-in-the-Field in London on a warm summer evening to hear a classical music concert. As we sat down, the eastern window caught my eye. The window is a kind of stained glass without the stain—clear, etched glass with a tilted oval in the center, a modern depiction of the tilted head of Jesus on the cross. It has been called one of the most significant pieces of religious art commissioned in modern times. As the sun went down, the musicians walked in silence into the candlelit sanctuary.

> *What kinds of beauty "stop you in your tracks"? What do you find most pleasing?*

Then the five musicians began playing, first Mozart's *Divertimento in D Major,* then Pachelbel's *Canon in D,* followed by Bach's "Jesu, Joy of Man's Desiring," and ended with Vivaldi's *The Four Seasons*—all four seasons. We listened in a state of rapture. When they played the last note we looked at each other and were both weeping. Why? We were not sad; quite the opposite. We wept because we had been touched by beauty. The beauty of the church, the glass window piece, and the sounds of musical notes arranged exquisitely created an epiphanic experience. When we encounter beauty, we tend to say, "Wow!"

GOODNESS

"Beauty," said Dallas Willard, "is goodness made manifest to the senses." What is goodness? Goodness is that which works for the benefit or betterment of another. If, as Aquinas said, beauty is that which, when seen, pleases, then goodness is that which, when experienced, benefits. That which is good makes us better, heals us, restores us, improves us, strengthens us, and makes us right, perhaps when we were wrong. We are naturally drawn to goodness, and unless there is some brokenness in us we are naturally repelled by evil.

I love to hear stories about people who do good things. My friend Shane and some of his friends restored an abandoned lot in a depressed neighborhood by turning it into a lovely park. The city of Philadelphia tried to prevent them from doing it because it belonged to the city. They pressed on, and when the park was completed, the community came out to enjoy it. It was beautiful, and it was an act of goodness. The community rallied, and the city officials came and saw it and changed their minds.

Human goodness has one important characteristic: love. To love is to will the good of another. The finest exposition on love is 1 Corinthians 13:4-8: "Love is patient; love is kind; love is not envious or boastful or arrogant or rude. It does not insist on its own way; it is not irritable or resentful; it does not rejoice in wrongdoing, but rejoices in the truth. It bears all things, believes all things, hopes all things, endures all things. Love never ends." Though this text is often heard at weddings, it is not about marriage only. It is an explanation of what love looks like. Paul is defining all that is good and all that is not. Patience is good. It benefits those who are patient and those around them. That is true of kindness, of forbearance, of faith, of hope, and of endurance. On the other hand, envy is harmful to those who are envious and to those around them. That is true of boasting, arrogance, resentment, and rejoicing in wrongdoing.

And all the things that are good are also beautiful. I saw an act of kindness on a plane ride. An older couple had been assigned separate seats, and a man willingly gave up his aisle seat in order for them to sit together. It made me smile because his kindness was good. To love is to will the good of another, but it is also an act of beauty. That which is *not* good we call evil. Though it is a bit corny, I once heard a preacher say evil is *live* spelled backward. Anything that goes against what helps us live is therefore evil. And evil is always ugly. Think again about the list in 1 Corinthians 13: when you see arrogance, you see ugliness. It is also working against truth. When we encounter goodness, we tend to say, "Thanks!"

TRUTH

The final transcendental longing we have is for truth. We often ask, "Is it true?" We innately want to know if something is right, if it's true. Something is true if it is aligned with reality. Something is false if it is not aligned with reality. Reality is what you bump into when you are wrong. Reality—the way things actually are—may not always be believed, but eventually it will prevail. Reality does not budge. So according to our definitions of these terms we could say: truth is that which, when encountered, *works*. Nutritionists and dietitians tell us it is a good idea to eat a balanced diet. It is either true or false, regardless of who is saying it. Homes used to be built using lead in the pipes and asbestos for insulation. Both, as it turns out, are deadly. Truth doesn't change.

Truth is not merely the right historical account of something. Truth is woven into reality. This is why a fictional story can tell the truth. The fable known as "The Tortoise and the Hare" is one of the most well-known stories. It tells a basic truth: slow and steady wins the race. The fable, while fictional, tells a truth. As C. S. Lewis wrote, "The story of Christ is simply a true myth: a myth working on us in the same way as the others, but with this tremendous difference that *it really happened*."

Those who engage in apologetics, or defending the faith, or trying to convince people Jesus is Lord, often find themselves using *truth* as their defense. While I believe the Christian convictions about Jesus (for example, he was the Son of God who rose from the dead) are true, I am not drawn to Jesus only by truth. I am drawn to Jesus by his beauty and his goodness. Still, truth is an essential aspect of our lives. We need it to build a good and beautiful life. We can easily be deceived, but when we encounter truth, we tend to say, "Yes!"

The late theologian Hans Urs von Balthasar wrote that beauty "will not allow herself to be separated and banned from her two sisters," goodness and truth. Beauty, goodness, and truth are, like the Trinity, of one essence. When all three—beauty, goodness, and truth—are aligned, you are dealing with reality at its deepest level. It resonates in your heart, where transformation takes place. If you bump up against truth, for example, it's also likely to be good and beautiful. They refuse, as Balthasar wrote, to be separated from one another. The transcendentals of beauty, goodness, and truth are not merely ideas, concepts, or speculations at the whim of our tastes. They are at the heart of reality.

A BRIEF WORD ON SUBJECTIVITY AND RELATIVITY

During the twentieth century a new narrative began to emerge, and it eventually became the dominant narrative by the end of the century. The narrative goes like this: beauty, goodness, and truth are subjective and relative. Beauty is in the eye of the beholder. We cannot know truth for certain. And no one is truly good. A more contemporary sentiment among the millennial generation goes like this: I will find my own truth.

Subjectivity refers to how judgment is shaped by inward influences (personal opinions and feelings) rather than outer influences.

Beauty is, to a degree, subjective. It is *partially* in the eye of the beholder. Our own tastes, shaped by our culture and our experiences, allow us to see more beauty in some things than in others. One of my friends loves the paintings of Picasso. I am not drawn to Picasso the way she is; I prefer the paintings of Rembrandt. But there is beauty in both. This is true of the beauty we experience in music, food, literature, home decor, and architecture. I visited Graceland, the former home of Elvis Presley, which is preserved exactly as it was when Elvis died. His famous Jungle Room has green shag carpeting from floor to ceiling. Not my style, but I imagine Elvis thought it beautiful. To be beautiful, something must contain the previously mentioned characteristics (clarity, harmony, tone, and so on). Individual tastes will vary.

Truth and goodness are said to be relative. Relativity has to do with relation and proportion. Goodness does have a measure of relativity. Some actions are good (writing a thank-you note), and some are *very* good (donating an organ). Truth also is relative in the sense that some truths affect us more than others. It is true that two plus two equals four. A deeper truth is that it's better to give than to receive. The important thing to note is that we are living in what has been called a *postmodern* culture that has abandoned beauty, goodness, and truth as essential elements of life. I believe we desperately need all three.

I do not want a postmodern dentist: "Well, I'm not sure about your tooth, because we can't be sure we know what is wrong. My diagnosis is subjective." No, I want a dentist who has a grasp on the reality of my tooth. Yes, we all have to make interpretations, and we can all be wrong (doctors once bled people to heal them). The truth will always prevail because reality is what we bump into when we are wrong. However, we can also be *right*. I want my mechanic and the guy who builds bridges and the woman who performs open-heart surgery to be right.

In the same way, we need a story that is beautiful, good, and true in order to live a beautiful, good, and true life. Next we will examine how a story can (and cannot) be beautiful, good, and true.

CONNECTING OUR STORIES WITH
THE BEAUTIFUL, GOOD, AND TRUE STORY

I met a man who watches *The Lord of the Rings* movies every night. When he told me this I pushed back: "Every night?" He said that when he gets off work he goes home, fixes his dinner, turns on the movie, and watches until he gets sleepy. He stops the movie and resumes in the same spot the next night. I was stunned by this, but in a way I understand. Great stories filled with adventure, with an epic battle of good versus evil, where tragedy ends in triumph, do something to our soul nothing else can.

We are creatures with a mystery in our heart that is bigger than ourselves. We may think we can find ultimate pleasure, satisfaction, and meaning in alcohol, sex, money, or power, but in reality those

Is there a movie you enjoy watching again and again? What do you find appealing about that movie?

have never satisfied anyone. They are too small for our massive souls. We were designed to take part in a divine drama, an epic story. We were made not merely to hear it but *to be in it*. We are, indeed, stories. But in truth we are not the protagonists of the real story, the story we long to take part in. God is the hero of the only story that will satisfy us.

The thesis of this book is that there is a *magnificent story*, which is the most important thing happening on this earth. It is our only hope as individuals, communities, countries, and a species. But for a variety of reasons the gospel message we often hear, the story often told, is shrunken and distorted. This is why we see so many frustrated, disappointed Christians. It is not that they are bad people, but they have never heard the magnificent story in its fullness.

Hearing the good news of the gospel is similar to crying over the beauty of heavenly music. Experiencing the good news of the gospel is similar to feeling glad when we see someone perform an unexpected act of kindness for a stranger. The greatest news is that

this is what *God* is like. To discover this we need to look at the story—
the gospel—through the lenses of beauty, goodness, and truth.

My friend Trevor stated it well: "In order to see beauty, goodness,
and truth, I have to have humble eyes." Our eyes can be humble
only when we get ourselves out of the way and focus on the beauty
all around us. And we see God best when we learn to see and experience beauty, goodness, and truth. When we see them we get a
glimpse of God. We not only see them, but we hear them, we smell
them, we touch them, and we taste them. God gave us all of our
senses—physical and spiritual—to feel God's love.

God sings his love to you in birdsong. God smiles at you in
maple trees. God charms you with the color green. He gave you
eyes to see sunsets, ears to hear rainfall, a nose to smell a rose. God's
massive love appears in the small fragments. God is loving you in
these moments, even if you don't know it.

BEAUTY AND SUFFERING: THE CELLIST OF SARAJEVO

From 1992 to 1995 the world witnessed one of the worst civil
conflicts, the Bosnian War. Three factions, each tied to a religion
(Orthodox Serbs, Catholic Croats, and Muslim Bosniaks), began
attacking one another in a struggle for power after the breakup
of Yugoslavia. The Serbs, backed by the Yugoslavian army, at-
tacked the Croats and Bosniaks, but the latter two united and
fought back. In the end no one was innocent of the bloodshed.
Over 100,000 people were killed, 2.2 million people were dis-
placed, and it is estimated that over 12,000 women—mostly
Muslim—were raped.

In the midst of the ugliness and the suffering, beauty emerged to
offer a different story. As the mortar shells rained down on Sarajevo,
a musician from Bosnia and Herzegovina named Vedran Smailović
did the only thing he knew to do: he played his cello. In the midst

of the destruction of buildings and the killing of his family and friends, Vedran played his cello—in full formal attire—alone in the ruins and in the streets, even though there was relentless sniper fire.

During the conflict no one knew when or where he would play, but as soon as someone heard him playing, the crowds grew. Grieving and starving, the people gathered to listen. Why? As Smailović said, "They were hungry, but they still had soul." In the midst of tragedy, his music echoed from another world, a place where beauty, goodness, and truth reside. Through Smailović—an instrument of God, I believe—the people found hope and healing.

As he played his cello in the ruined city during the forty-four-month siege, Smailović inspired people around the world. Singer Joan Baez sat in solidarity with him as he played on the streets. Composer David Wilde wrote a piece for cello in his honor: "The Cellist of Sarajevo," played by Yo-Yo Ma. Smailović became a symbol of how beauty stands in resistance to the madness of war. Aleksandr Solzhenitsyn, in a speech he gave after winning the Nobel Prize, said, "If the too obvious, too straight branches of Truth and Good are crushed or amputated and cannot reach the light—yet perhaps the . . . unexpected branches of Beauty will make their way through

Vedran Smailović playing the cello in Sarajevo

and soar up *to that very place* and in this way perform the work of all three." Perhaps Dostoevsky was right when he said, "Beauty will save the world."

WHAT IS AT STAKE?

Our world is in search of a magnificent story. Many people are hungering for something that will provide answers to their deepest longings. Like my daughter Hope, many of us want to take part in a great story. No one wants to live a lame life, yet it seems many people are doing just that, including Christians. Our magnificent story has been reduced, shrunken into a tame, manageable story failing to create magnificent lives.

What is the most compelling vision in your life? What makes it compelling for you?

We need a vision. We need the true Christian story.

W E ARE MADE FOR A BEAUTIFUL, GOOD, AND TRUE story. If you are like me, you have not spent a lot of time thinking about beauty or goodness or truth—even though they are a large part of our lives. Yet we are constantly evaluating things on the basis of their beauty ("Wow, that home is beautiful"), their goodness ("Is ice cream good or bad for us?"), and their truth ("Is that politician telling the truth or just being self-serving?"). The practice for this week, along with other practices throughout this book, is aimed at helping you become more aware of the beauty, goodness, and truth all around us.

We become more *aware* of beauty, goodness, and truth by being more *intentional*. A journal is a great way to become more intentional and to reflect on the impact of the practice. If you are able, buy a nice journal to write in (though a notebook will do). This week we are focusing on beauty. Be on the lookout for beauty and write about it.

Another way to do this exercise is to keep a photo journal. Perhaps you can take pictures of what you see and either put them in a journal or make a file in your phone. You can title the file "Beauty I Have Seen." Or if you see something beautiful in a magazine, you could cut it out and paste it into an actual journal.

For many, beauty is most clearly revealed in creation (most easily through sight). For example, you will likely *see* trees and flowers, green grass, a blue sky, a bird soaring. But also be open to beautiful *smells* (honeysuckle), *tastes* (chocolate), *sounds* (rainfall), and *touch* (a cool breeze). The human voice can produce incredible beauty. Each year at our annual spiritual formation conference at Friends University, our student choir, the Singing Quakers, enters the auditorium and surrounds the audience. They then sing beautiful sacred music. I look out at the crowd as I sit on the stage, and energy, power, and light shine on the audience members' faces, many of them weeping, nearly everyone smiling. Remember, beauty is "that which, when seen, pleases."

Beauty (as well as goodness and truth) is not ultimate (the last) but penultimate (the second to the last). The point is not the beautiful sunset, the violin concerto, or the painting. That would make the beautiful thing ultimate, thus making it an idol. Beauty is designed to point to something else—God. God is the Creator of all things, so when we experience beauty it is right and good to thank God for it, as God is the ultimate. So in your journal find a way of giving thanks for the beauty you have experienced. Let "wow" be your way of giving thanks.

A final word: do not worry about when you do this exercise. Some find it best to do this in the evening since the day is still fresh in their minds. Others are better able to start their day with this exercise, as they might be tired in the evening.

FALLING FOR SHRUNKEN STORIES

Each tree is known by its own fruit.

LUKE 6:44

I GREW UP AS A CHRISTMAS and Easter Methodist. Our family called ourselves Christians, but it was not an important part of our lives. I found church boring. When I turned eighteen, something happened to me. Though my life was outwardly good, I was inwardly empty. So I began a spiritual quest. I wanted to connect to God but did not know how. I shared this hunger with my close friend Jeff, and it turned out he felt the same way. Jeff reminded me that his family had also gone to our church, so he suggested we go to church that next Sunday.

The church service felt cold, and the sermon was dry. We noticed in the bulletin that on Wednesday they had a "seeker's meeting" where we could learn what the church teaches. So we decided to attend.

GOSPEL STORY 1: THE DO-GOOD-WORKS GOSPEL

Jeff and I were excited to learn about God: Would this be the answer to our prayers? The minister welcomed us, along with ten others, into the parlor. After a brief introduction, the minister began sharing what he and those in his church believed. He started out with a shocking statement: "Jesus was not divine. He was not the Son of God any more than any of us are sons and daughters of God. Jesus was a great teacher, as were Socrates and Gandhi."

The room was silent. "But the Bible says that Jesus rose from the dead," I said.

"Yes, it does, young man. But you see, the Bible is merely mythology," he explained. "It was written in ancient times, when people created myths about the gods to explain the universe. We in the twentieth century have progressed from those days. We have science, and that has replaced superstition."

"So," my friend Jeff asked, "what is the point of Christianity?"

"It is trying to be a good person and to do good things. Trying to live an ethical life, to right society's wrongs, and to engage in social justice causes," the minister said.

It was a puzzling meeting. I took a lot of notes, and at the end the minister gave all of us a free copy of his book, *The Endless Search*, explaining to us that God, as well as life's meaning, could never be grasped. "Life is an endless search, and you never reach any kind of certainty."

Jeff and I sat in my car afterward and talked for an hour as the snow fell. Finally, I said to Jeff, "What do you think about all of the things he said?"

"Seems like a waste of time to me," Jeff said.

"Me too," I agreed.

THE FALSE NARRATIVE

The story I heard from my minister can be summed up like this: God is distant and uninvolved, so it's up to us make the world better.

Dallas Willard called this "the gospel on the left." It is most common in churches that are labeled "liberal." People are attracted to these churches because of their emphasis on reason and social justice. Jesus becomes a compelling figure because he taught about love and kindness, about justice and mercy for the least and the lost, and ultimately gave his own life for this cause. Jesus' miracles cannot be taken as literal, but must be seen as symbolic.

While reason is a gift, science has benefited humankind in massive ways, and social justice is what God wants and what we all must strive for, those three things are not strong enough to sustain the human soul. This is because this gospel, which I call the "good works gospel," relies too heavily on human beings. It shrinks the gospel to goodness, leaving out the truth of Jesus' resurrected life, ignoring the beauty of sacrifice and redemption.

While both liberals and conservatives argue on the basis of the *good* and the *true*, they do not have the power of the *beautiful* to transform. Social ethicists may speak about doing the right thing, but they fail to deliver the kind of healing and transformation that makes social reform stay reformed. They cannot forgive sins, nor can they heal the broken or offer a genuine ground for compassion.

This shrunken story has had its day, particularly in the twentieth century. Two world wars and countless other wars, terrorism, and school shootings indicate that we have not progressed as much as we thought. This story is too small. It is centered on humans, who are puny. It had its chance and is found wanting. Our souls cannot survive on goodness alone, which isn't sustainable or redemptive anyway. It is a well-meaning but shrunken version of the full gospel that ignited the first Christians.

GOSPEL STORY 2: THE SHAMING AND SCARY GOSPEL

Jesus made himself known to me not long after my experience at the "good works" church. Since I had been on a religious quest for almost a year, I was open to anything that might take away my sense of emptiness. The summer after graduation I spent a lot of time with a part-time street evangelist named Pat. We read the Bible together, and he gave me a copy of C. S. Lewis's *Mere Christianity*. Near the end of the summer, I was nearly persuaded that Jesus was the Son of God who rose from the dead. I was fascinated by Jesus and was struck by the story of his resurrection, and after a few weeks (and the work of the Holy Spirit) I came to believe Jesus really did rise from the dead. Maybe. So I knelt by my bed and prayed, "Jesus, if you are really the risen Christ, then do something so I know it's true."

Beginning the next day, and every day after that for the next two weeks, things began happening. When I read the Bible, I actually understood it. When I prayed, things actually happened as I had asked—or better. At the end of the two-week experiment I decided I was a Christian. I didn't know a lot about Christians, but I knew they liked jewelry, so I went to a Christian bookstore and bought a fish necklace. I didn't know at the time what the fish meant, but it seemed the right way to honor this newfound relationship with Jesus. I awoke each day eager to spend it with my Savior, Teacher, Lord, and Friend.

I felt an inner warmth and a spring in my step that I had never felt before. I broke the news to my friend Jeff, and amazingly the same thing happened to him. I told my parents, and they seemed surprised and a little concerned, but also pleased. Jeff and I formed a Bible study consisting of the two of us, along with my most Christian friend, Tim, who had given me a Bible a year earlier. Tim was happy I had found Jesus. The three of us invited some of our friends to join us, and amazingly they did. We read from the Gospels and talked about the resurrection of Jesus and the change in our own lives. Several of our friends also became Christians. This Christian thing was a blast!

A few weeks later I was off to college for my freshman year. I was so new to the faith that when a guy I knew from high school saw my necklace and asked if I was a Christian, it took me a moment to say yes. When he found out, he invited me to a campus fellowship gathering. My childhood church experiences were not pleasant, so I was reluctant to go. But I was pleased to find out that there were a lot of people like me who had been gently ambushed by Jesus and enjoyed being together.

I was growing in my faith day by day, and Jesus was very real to me. Then I met a guy—I will call him Fred—who worked for a parachurch ministry for college students. He was not a student but was on campus to minister to them. When he found out I was a new Christian he decided to find out if I had come to *saving faith* (his term) in the right way. Over coffee he asked if I had prayed the "sinner's prayer." I told him I hadn't. I didn't even know what it was. If I had not done so I was not saved, he said. I asked what he meant by "saved." He told me that salvation was the promise of eternal life in heaven when I died and that I could not be saved unless I prayed the right prayer, the right way.

I asked him why this prayer was so important. Fred explained that I (and everyone living) was a rotten sinner who deserved to burn in hell forever but that Jesus—by grace—took my punishment for me. If I admitted I was a rotten sinner who deserved hell and then professed my faith in Jesus' death for me, I could be saved.

There was no other way to be saved. I told him I had spent the summer reading the Gospels and had found Jesus to be astonishing and wonderful. I explained I had asked Jesus to enter my life, and to do it in a way that made sure I knew he was real. Jesus did as I asked, and was now someone who interacted with me daily.

"That's a nice story, but you're not saved. If you died tonight, you would go to hell," Fred explained. Alarmed and confused and afraid, I asked, "What? Why?"

"Because you are a despicable sinner," he said with a deadpan gaze. Feeling I had nothing to lose, despicable me decided to say the prayer. He handed me a tract that had the prayer printed out, which made it easy. So I prayed it out loud, and when I finished I looked at Fred, who seemed happy about my decision to say the prayer—the *right* one. In fact, I would later learn I had become another number on his list of the "decisions" he had led people to make.

"So, am I saved?" I asked Fred.

"Yes. For now. But you can *lose* your salvation," he said.

"How?" I asked.

"By having unconfessed sin in your life. If you sin and don't confess it, it remains on the ledger," he explained.

"I have a ledger?" I asked.

"Yes, and so does everyone."

"So what can I do?" I asked.

"Keep short accounts with God."

"I have an account with God?" I asked.

"Yes. Every time you sin it goes on your record, and you have to confess it in order for it to be taken off."

"Every sin? Forever?" I asked.

"Yes. If you have even one unconfessed sin, you can go to hell."

"Wow. That seems impossible. So how am I going to manage this?" I asked.

"Well, for starters, stop sinning."

"But you said I am a rotten sinner. Isn't sinning what sinners do?" I pled.

"Well, yes, but try to cut the number down. Be sure to confess any sin you commit. I will give you a secret practice that will help you."

Ooh. Secret practice. This was getting interesting.

"It is called *spiritual breathing*," Fred said. "What you do is focus on not sinning, but when you do, confess it right away. Breathe out your confession. Then breathe in your absolution, your forgiveness. That is spiritual breathing. And it is the best way I have found to keep short accounts with God."

So I began practicing spiritual breathing. It soon turned into spiritual *panting*, and eventually became spiritual *hyperventilating*. I was so focused on not sinning that I think I sinned even more. What had been a tender and trusting few months with Jesus had now become a fearful and anxious trial. Fred's story was intriguing: rotten sinners, an angry God, a sacrificial Son, and the constant battle to make it to heaven in the end. I accepted this story that day, and for the next twelve years it was *my story*. Others around me were telling the same story, so I assumed it was true. I lived in that story through college, seminary, and into the ministry.

Then one day I came to the realization I hated being a Christian. I no longer wanted to be in the story. I told God I was leaving the ministry. I felt I would be happier as anything other than a minister. I gave Jesus one last season in my life to make a change. Jesus took me up on the offer. As he had done before, things started to change immediately. God used people and wonderful books to tell me something I never thought I would hear: being a Christian was not my problem. The problem was the story, Fred's story. It was neither good nor beautiful nor true.

THE FALSE NARRATIVE

The gospel of Fred can be summed up like this: you are bad, God is mad, but Jesus took your beating. So try harder and you might make it to heaven.

This way of explaining the atonement (atonement means becoming one with God) was not the original gospel of the early church. The fourth-century theologian Athanasius emphasized Jesus' victory over sin and death, for example. There were many ways to explain the saving work of Jesus, and because there is so much about us that needs deliverance we need every theory of the atoning work of Jesus we can find. The early Christians faced martyrdom with confidence because they believed that the oppressive powers we face had been defeated. They believed Jesus rose from the dead and now rules the world as the King. Fred's version of the gospel can be found in church history on a few occasions, but it never became the central way of explaining the revolution started by Jesus.

Is Fred's presentation of the gospel familiar to you? When put in these stark terms, what is your reaction to it?

Then, in the late nineteenth century, the revivals began, and one way to tell the story became the *only way* to tell the story, which was reduced to a sales pitch. It was a simple way to talk about salvation: you are bad and God is mad, but Jesus took your blame, so believe in his sacrifice and you get to go to heaven down the road. By the mid-twentieth century, this gospel became the dominant way of framing the Christian story for most evangelical Protestants. In fact, in one of my classes at the university, I polled the students, asking if this version of the gospel was the one they were told growing up. Fifteen out of fifteen said yes.

WHY THESE STORIES HAVE SUCH STAYING POWER

Why are these two stories so dominant?

First, each of these shrunken stories contains a measure of truth. We *are* sinners. Jesus *did* die for us. Scientific progress *has* been a great blessing to humans. We *should* make the world better. They are convincing because they contain a measure of truth.

Second, the people who preach or teach these shriveled stories might have wonderful motives, with love for Jesus warming their hearts. Fred, for example, had a wonderful heart and compassion for people. He simply told the story he had been told. My minister wanted to help people. He learned his gospel, I later learned, in seminary in the 1950s, and was simply telling the truth as best he understood it. Just because we can see where these stories fall short does not make us better or smarter or more Christian people.

Third, and perhaps most important, they have staying power because they allow us to stay in control. It's up to me to save the world. I like when things are about me. In the other story, I can control God by having the right understanding of my depravity, the right view of the atonement, and the right prayer to bring me into heaven. It is all about us and our control. Both turn out to be individualistic and leave no room for mystery and community. Worst of all, they make God small and mean.

ARE THESE STORIES TRUE?

Both gospels contain a measure of truth. The social gospel can be found on the lips of Jesus and in the pen of Paul. But compassion and justice are meant to be the fruit of becoming part of a larger, better, more compelling story. If Jesus was not raised from the dead, Paul said, we are still in our sins and our faith is in vain. Regarding the shaming story, explaining the work of Jesus on the cross in this way has a measure of truth. Proclaiming that Jesus' death on the cross paid the penalty for our sins is a true statement. But when you make one story the *only* story, you end up telling a story that is no longer true. Let me explain.

Building the wrong Roman road. Recently two ladies from a local church knocked on my door on a Saturday afternoon. They handed me a tract titled "You Can Get to Heaven from Kansas." They asked, "Are you a Christian?" I said I was. Then they pulled the tract back, saying, "You don't need this." I asked if I could have it nonetheless, and they said yes. When I looked inside I immediately saw it was the shaming gospel. The tract contained four "points on a map," followed by verses from Romans.

1. Realize you are a sinner. (Romans 3:23)
2. Realize there is a penalty for your sin. (Romans 6:23: "For the wages of sin is death.")
3. Realize Jesus paid the penalty. (Romans 5:8)
4. Repent of your sin and receive Jesus as Savior. (Romans 10:13)

Each of the four verses from Romans is taken out of context in order to fit the story the tract writers want to tell.

The first point in this story is to realize you are a sinner. Romans 3:23 says we are all sinners. But the context is the debate about whether Jews have priority over Gentiles (the central issue in the whole epistle). Paul explains that we are all on equal ground: we all—Gentile and Jew—have not been able to find justification through the law. We have all sinned. But this is the not the point of the story. The story Paul is telling is that God has established a new way: confidence in the risen Jesus.

The second point is to realize you are destined to hell because of your sin, and Romans 6:23, according to the tract, says so. The context of Romans 6 is not about hell; the word *hell* (even the concept) never occurs. The context of Romans 6 is whether Christians can still sin but be protected by grace (v. 1). Paul answers it in two ways. In verses 1-14, he explains those who are in Christ have died and risen with Jesus, so we no longer have any business with sin; it is not who we are now. In verses 15-23, Paul answers the question from another angle: Why should we sin, when sin enslaves and ultimately kills us? Sin's payment is death. Paul is stating something true (it aligns with reality). Sin always produces death. He is not talking about hell later but about life now.

The third point, that Jesus died for you, is built on Romans 5:8. Taken at face value, it is true; Jesus died for all of us. But just as Romans 6 never talks about hell, Romans 5 never talks about heaven. Jesus died to save us—now. He rescued us from the dominion of darkness (Colossians 1:13). For Paul, salvation has already begun. Jesus has already saved us. He reconciled us to God through the cross, but salvation comes through the resurrection. Two verses after Romans 5:8, Paul writes, "For if while we were enemies, we were *reconciled* to God through the *death* of his Son, much more surely, having been reconciled, will we be *saved by his life*" (Romans 5:10, italics added). We were reconciled by his death (not by our faith in it) but saved by his life! For Paul and the early church, the resurrection of Jesus was the central reality that changed everything.

The final point is predicated on Acts 20:21—namely, that we must first repent to God and then have faith in Jesus. The Greek word for *repent* is *metanoeō*, which means "to change your mind." We usually interpret *repent* to mean "shape up," "change your ways," or "intend to be righteous." That fits nicely with the shaming gospel. But it is not what Paul intended. Acts 20:21, contextually, is about how Paul summed up his message: change your mind about God, and put your confidence in the risen Jesus. Again, this passage has nothing to do with heaven or hell.

The last verse used to tell the shaming gospel is Romans 10:13, stating that everyone who calls on the name of Jesus will be saved. At face value, this is true. But the context is not about heaven when you die but whether Jews have an advantage over Gentiles. If we back up one verse we read: "For there is no distinction between Jew and Greek; the same Lord is Lord of all and is generous to all who call on him" (Romans 10:12). Again, salvation is not something that happens at death but a quality of life experienced now, the moment you call on Jesus' name. The whole world—and our whole life—is radically different once we believe that Jesus rose from the dead.

When it comes to interpreting the Bible, St. Augustine wisely said, "Whoever, then, thinks that he understands the Holy Scriptures, or any part of them, but puts such an interpretation upon them as does not tend to build up this twofold love of God and our neighbor, does not yet understand them as he ought." We read a passage rightly if our interpretation leads us to love God more fully, as well as our neighbor and ourselves.

> *What is your reaction to the explanation of the misinterpretation of the four-step gospel? What does this misinterpretation lead to? What is at stake in getting it wrong?*

IS IT GOOD OR BEAUTIFUL?

If it is not true, it will be neither good nor beautiful, because you cannot have one without the other. Goodness is that which is beneficial. When you encounter goodness, the response is gratitude, a deep sense of thanksgiving. Both gospels contain a measure of goodness. The social gospel is about making the world better, which is good. But it's up to us to make it happen. And that is not good. The shaming gospel is about Jesus dying for us, which is good. But it leaves an angry Father, who is still mad at us, and does not mention the work of the Holy Spirit. And that is not good. Neither story is truly and deeply good. At best they incite fear and servitude.

Finally, neither story is beautiful, inspiring awe and wonder. When we encounter beauty we ought to say "wow." The only story large enough for the human soul is the story that stops us in our tracks with wonder; it melts our cold hearts with the warmth of love and goodness; and it is sturdy enough to build our lives on, now and forever. Hans Urs von Balthasar said, "*Within* the beautiful—the whole person quivers." We need a story that makes us quiver, not with fear but with delight. We need a story so big that we will never be able to grasp it, so vast that it can handle the darkness of evil and suffering, so immense that it can make sense of cancer and terrorism.

WHAT IS AT STAKE IN GETTING IT WRONG?

These two shriveled stories share the following:

- Neither is the story of the early Christians.
- Neither leads us to love God, ourselves, and others with our entire heart, soul, mind, and strength (the Great Commandment).
- Neither starts in the right place.
- Neither includes the Trinity as one in heart and mission.
- Neither views creation as a portal to God.
- Neither sees Jesus in his complete form.
- Neither leads naturally to discipleship.

Keep in mind that while pieces of these gospels were familiar to the first Christians, neither were preached by them. To be sure, the early Christians not only did not deny the resurrection, they built everything on its reality. And they did not, as in Fred's gospel, put their focus on Jesus as a victim but as a victor, seeing the cross as necessary, but mainly to establish a new creation through the resurrection.

In the social gospel, God is distant (if God exists at all). It is not a story that makes me want to love God. In the shaming gospel, God the Father is angry. This does not lead me to love God but to be afraid of God. It is not a story about a community of loving Persons (the Trinity) who are on a mission of love to invite everyone into their community. This story alone can lead me to love God with every ounce of my being.

These stories are too small because they start with us. The social gospel puts humans at the center of the universe. Humankind is the generator of science, progress, and justice. The shaming gospel also starts with us: "*you* are a sinner." Salvation is about getting *us* into heaven. The early church's gospel was about the availability of heaven *now*, not because of anything we did, and not just because of the cross, but because Jesus rebooted the entire creation.

What is appealing— and unappealing—about starting the story with us?

Finally, neither of these stories leads people to be Jesus' disciples or apprentices. The social gospel sees Jesus as a dead teacher, not a living teacher in whose school we can enroll today. The shaming gospel sees Jesus only as a sin manager, not someone who defeated death and has rescued the world and transferred it into a new kingdom that awaits a new creation.

There is good news: it's a magnificent story that can woo us, wow us, humble us, and inspire us to love God, ourselves, and others. It is an ancient story. I will tell it the best I can in the following chapters. It is a story about the Trinity as a loving community, about creation as a proclamation of the glory of God and a sign of God's love, about humans bearing the image of God whose likeness has been tarnished by sin but designed for goodness and relationship with God, about the incarnation as the coming of a King and his unshakable kingdom, about a divine rescue mission, and finally about the restoration of all things. It is the story we all long for, the story we were meant to enter.

Soul Training Exercise
GOODNESS

O BSERVATION IS A POWERFUL PRACTICE. But being mindful is a challenge. We have the weapons of mass distraction (we call them smartphones) that beckon us to look at them. This week the challenge is to be aware of the goodness you see around you. If you are a journal keeper, continue putting entries into your beauty, goodness, and truth journal. This week please focus on goodness. Goodness is that which is beneficial, that which makes something better. There are countless acts of goodness all around us. When I see an older couple holding hands, I am seeing the goodness of faithfulness, of love, and of endurance. When I see someone make a sacrifice for the benefit of another, I am seeing goodness. Recently, I was able to go to a cabin to write. The couple who owns it, Jim and Jenny Knight, graciously offered me their place for a week. Jenny's father, John, comes by to check on me. These are acts of goodness.

As with beauty, when you see it and write about it, make sure to give thanks to God for it. God designed us with a need for goodness and to be good ourselves; we were made to do justice and love kindness and to walk humbly with our God. That is goodness made manifest, and it comes from the heart of our Maker. Look for acts of love. Because we interact with people much of the time, we will also see moments of kindness, hospitality, concern, and good listening. However, I must add a caveat:

we are likely to see some ugliness. In this fallen world we will likely see anger, meanness, gossip, and even quarreling. If you encounter these, write about them as well. They are goodness turned upside down. Use this awareness as a chance to pray for those experiencing the absence of goodness.

PARTICIPATING IN THE TRINITY

*There is one body, and one Spirit, even as
ye are called in one hope of your calling; One Lord,
one faith, one baptism, One God and Father of all,
who is above all, and through all, and in you all.*

EPHESIANS 4:4-6 KJV

ACCORDING TO LEGEND, the man we know as St. Patrick was responsible for ridding Ireland of snakes in the fifth century. For most people, Patrick inspired wearing green, eating corned beef and cabbage, parades, and throwing a big party on March 17. More important than the snakes and the parades, Patrick is credited with saving Ireland *spiritually*. It is said that Patrick used the shamrock as a symbol to explain the Trinity to unbelievers—God is one God in three Persons. Patrick would hold up a shamrock and say to his hearers, "Is it one leaf or three?"

"It is both one leaf and three," they would reply.

"And so it is with God," he would conclude.

It is a great illustration, but it does not fully explain the mystery of the Trinity. We can understand the concept, but we cannot fully grasp the Trinity. That can also be said of the transcendentals of beauty, goodness, and truth. We can define beauty as "that which, when seen, pleases." But there is something going on at a deeper level—an exchange—that is a mystery. This is because both the Trinity and the transcendentals are known and experienced only relationally. Jesus is Son because there is a Father; the Spirit is the love between the Father and the Son.

The transcendentals, like the Trinity, are also three in one. If you experience beauty, you also experience truth and goodness. If you see the Father, you see Jesus and the Spirit. The three transcendentals have been compared to the members of the Trinity. We see the beauty of God the Father in creation. We see the goodness of the Son in his self-sacrifice. We see the truth of the Spirit in the way the Spirit leads us into all truth. And yet they are one. In the beginning God created the heavens and the earth, proclaiming, "Let there be light." But then we read how "the Spirit of God was hovering over the face of the waters" (Genesis 1:1-3 ESV). Finally, we read in Colossians 1:16, "All things have been created through him and for him," referring to Jesus.

THE BEGINNING OF THE MAGNIFICENT STORY

Three. One. Mysteries we know only relationally. We know beauty when it strikes, goodness when it inspires us, and truth when it is revealed to us. We pray and we baptize in the name of the Father, the Son, and the Holy Spirit. They are all a part of a magnificent story. In fact, there is no magnificent story without the Trinity. So let's begin at the beginning of the story. In the beginning.

"In the beginning when God . . ." (Genesis 1:1).

The magnificent story starts with the Storyteller. The story begins with the creation of the universe. God creates light and darkness, the heavens and the earth, water and land, fish and fowl, and all living things. Then God creates humans. But notice the word that somehow sneaks into the text: "Then God said, 'Let us make humankind in our image, according to our likeness'" (Genesis 1:26).

Let *us* make. Us. In a fiercely monotheistic religion like Judaism, how did the word *us* get in the opening text? Some scholars believe God was speaking to the heavenly host of angels. But I prefer to believe that *us* refers to the Trinity—the Father, the Son, and the Holy Spirit.

We learn that Jesus was the agent of creation: "All things came into being through him, and without him not one thing came into being" (John 1:3). Thus, I believe that the Trinity created the world. And us. And we were made "according to" God's likeness. The Trinity is the heart of everything. The fabric of the universe is trinitarian. The key to all life is the Trinity. In truth, God's divine plan for us is found in the Trinity. Mark McIntosh writes,

> The Spirit of truth guides Jesus's followers by conducting them farther and farther, beyond their present capacities, into the fullness of the Father's life, which is given away to Jesus and through Jesus to the world, all by the power of this same Spirit. In all this lies the origin of both Christian faith in God as Trinity *and of Christian spirituality as a participation in that trinitarian life.*

We were made for participation in trinitarian life. When Jesus told his apprentices to go and make disciples, "baptizing them in the name of the Father and of the Son and of the Holy Spirit" (Matthew 28:19), he was not talking about getting people wet but rather *immersing people in trinitarian reality.*

There is only one problem. And it is a massive one. The Trinity seems to have gone missing.

A TRINITARIAN DEFICIT DISORDER

A student of mine, Josiah Brown, oversees the student outreach team. He and some of our students go to youth groups to teach the youth about Christian spiritual formation. They talk about what formation is, about living as an apprentice of Jesus, and about the role of narratives in formation. Knowing many people have toxic God narratives, Josiah has come up with an interesting exercise. He writes "God" on the left side of a whiteboard and asks, "What words would you use to describe God?" They all assume Josiah is asking about God *the Father*, and he is.

The youth say things such as "mean," "angry," "all-powerful," and "distant." Josiah writes them beneath the word *God*. He then writes "Jesus" on the right side of the board and asks, "What words would you use to describe Jesus?" The youth say things such as "compassionate," "loving," "forgiving," "wise," and "powerful." Josiah then pauses, and quotes John 14:9: "Whoever has seen me has seen the Father."

What is your reaction to Josiah's illustration and point?

Josiah lets that linger in the air for a moment. Then he asks, "Isn't Jesus telling us that he and God the Father are like a mirror? If that is true, then why do we think of God the Father as angry and mean, and Jesus as compassionate and forgiving?"

Why, indeed.

The Trinity is an early church doctrine that proclaims God is in three Persons: Father, Son, and Holy Spirit. It was challenging for the first Christians to believe Jesus was God because they were Jewish, and a central tenet of Judaism is "the Lord our God is one." How can

God be *two*? Jesus alluded to his divinity many times, such as in John 14:9. He also said, "Very truly, I tell you, before Abraham was, I am" (John 8:58). When my evangelist friend, Pat, led me into the faith, he focused on that verse. He pointed out that Jesus was claiming to be God, first by saying that he existed before Abraham, and second, because he referred to himself as "I am," the name for himself that God gave to Moses. The Pharisees, it says in the next verse, picked up stones to kill Jesus because he had just committed blasphemy.

After the resurrection, Jesus' disciples began to see everything Jesus had said in a new way, and like the Roman centurion at the cross, they proclaimed, "Truly this man was God's Son!" (Matthew 27:54). So, God was both Father and Son. Then, as the centuries passed, Christians began to understand that the Holy Spirit was also a member of the Godhead. It would take a few gatherings of bishops to fine-tune the language we use for the Trinity. The Trinity is a great mystery on three levels. First, the Trinity is beyond our comprehension. We have no way to understand how God can be three and one at the same time. Second, the Trinity is amazing, thrilling, and compelling. God is three Persons, living in complete submission to one another, on a mission to draw the world into God's community. Wow. Third, the church has largely either forgotten the Trinity or twisted it into something hard to stomach.

TWO FALSE NARRATIVES

"There is no need for the Trinity" is the first false narrative. Though most Christians would never say this out loud, it is revealed in how they live. Theologian Karl Rahner wrote, "Christians are, in their practical life, almost mere 'monotheists.'" We would never know they believed in the Trinity, because nothing about their lives reflects trinitarian engagement. Perhaps they adopted the social gospel: God is seen as a distant and uninvolved old man in the sky.

Jesus is distant because he was a great teacher who got killed. And the Holy Spirit is a nonfactor. Or perhaps they adopted the shaming gospel, and since Jesus died on the cross and made heaven possible after death, they don't need the Father (he has been appeased), or Jesus (he did his job), or the Holy Spirit (who never made it into the story in the first place, unless they are Pentecostal or charismatic).

"Jesus is the asbestos suit that saves us from the white-hot wrath of God" is the second false narrative. This is the view of the Trinity implicit in the shaming gospel. God the Father, the divine monarch, the cosmic judge, is angry with us due to our sin and is going to annihilate us because of it. God the Son, kind and compassionate, offers to die in our place. The two are not on the same page. They are at odds. But the Father relents and lets the Son pay the price. All that matters to the Father is justice, and Jesus provides that. In this story there is no Trinity, only a duality (Father and Son, no Spirit). And these gods are at odds, therefore there is no Trinity because the Trinity, by definition, is *one.* This provides the answer to Josiah's question, "Why is it that we think of God the Father as angry and mean, and Jesus as compassionate and forgiving?"

These narratives have become dominant. Now we need to ask, are they beautiful, good, and true?

IS IT BEAUTIFUL AND GOOD?

Let's start with beauty. Beauty is "that which, when seen, pleases." I find these narratives unpleasant. Whether it's a narrative that lacks the practical need for a Trinity or one that views the Trinity as a family feud, I am not moved to say "wow." They lack beauty. Are they good? Goodness is that which, when experienced, benefits. I don't see the benefit of these narratives. An unnecessary Trinity is an unhelpful Trinity. And a Son who asks to take our punishment is noble and creates a sense of gratitude on our part but still leaves us with an angry Father. In the end, courtroom images do not inspire love, only relief. Both of these narratives fail the beauty and goodness test. That leaves us with a final question: Is it true?

TRUE NARRATIVE

One of the gifts John Wesley left the church is the *Quadrilateral*. The Wesleyan Quadrilateral refers to the four ways we come to know something as true: *Scripture* (what the Bible teaches), *tradition* (the teaching of the church through the centuries), *reason* (our rational capacity), and *experience* (the knowledge we have of something experientially). Just as I have proposed that if something is true it's usually beautiful and good, Wesley proposed that if something is true, it must also be biblically grounded, be in sync with church teaching, make sense to us rationally, and make sense in our own lives.

This is a good way to examine what we believe. To be certain, Wesley put the greatest weight on Scripture, less weight on tradition, and even less weight on reason and experience, because we are all capable of deception (as history and our own lives have shown). It is my intention to use the Quadrilateral when answering the question, is it true?

Scripture. One day a member of the Jehovah's Witnesses knocked on my door. I knew he was a Jehovah's Witness not because of his dress or manner but because of his method of evangelism, which was scripted. He asked if I was a Christian, and I said yes. He then said, "So, do you have a Bible, I presume?" I told him I did. He asked if I would get it. It was not nice of me, but I played along, knowing where he was going next. I returned with my Bible and he said, "So, Christians believe in the Trinity. But what is interesting is that the

Trinity is never mentioned in the Bible. Go ahead, look in your Bible and show me where it mentions the Trinity."

This is the common method Jehovah's Witnesses use to show that Christianity has it all wrong. And they are correct; the word *Trinity* is not in the Bible. The term came into existence only in the third century. But the Trinity is very much in the Bible. The most explicit is the passage in the Great Commission, "baptizing them in the name of the Father and of the Son and of the Holy Spirit" (Matthew 28:19). The Trinity actually first appears at the baptism of Jesus:

> When Jesus had been baptized, just as he came up from the water, suddenly the heavens were opened to him and he saw the Spirit of God descending like a dove and alighting on him. And a voice from heaven said, "This is my Son, the Be-loved, with whom I am well pleased." (Matthew 3:16-17)

The Son rises, the Spirit descends, and the voice of the Father speaks. The Father speaks the exact same words at Jesus' transfiguration (Matthew 17:5). Throughout the Gospels we see the Trinity in action. Jesus is led into the wilderness by the Spirit. Jesus constantly interacts with the Father, most notably in the Garden of Gethsemane and on the cross.

The epistles also speak of the Trinity (without using the word). The most direct passage is Galatians 4:6: "Because you are children, God has sent the Spirit of his Son into our hearts, crying, 'Abba! Father!'" Notice the work the Trinity is doing: drawing us into fellowship. God the *Father* sends the *Spirit* of *Jesus* into our hearts so we can cry out "Abba! Father!" The Spirit draws us into the loving members of the Trinity, where we find our place.

The Jehovah's Witness was right—the word *Trinity* is not in the Bible. But the reality of the Trinity is on every page of the New Testament. But what you will not find in the Bible is the shaming, scary story. Nowhere does it say, "The Father was full of wrath toward the people, but Jesus stepped in and took their place." In fact, what you do find is the opposite. God the Father was a full participant in giving up his own Son. Paul uses this reality to show the ongoing faithfulness, love, and generosity of God: "He who did not withhold his own Son, but gave him up for all of us, will he not with him also give us everything else?" (Romans 8:32). This narrative is the opposite of the shaming gospel. The Trinity was fully committed to the rescuing act of the cross. St. Bonaventure advocated gazing on the mystery of the Father's love hidden in Jesus on the cross. If we have the eyes to see it, the white-hot love of God—Father, Son, and Spirit—bursts into flames on the cross.

Tradition. This understanding of the Trinity was established in the church at the Council of Nicaea in AD 325. Bishops gathered at church councils to make decisions on crucial theological and doctrinal issues. They used a Greek word to describe the oneness of the Father and the Son: *homoousios*. It means "same in essence." The early church fought hard because this understanding of the Trinity has far-reaching consequences—namely, our entire relationship with God. Fifty years after the Council of Nicaea, this understanding of the Trinity as three in one, as fully united in all they do, was also taught by one of the church's greatest theologians, Gregory of Nyssa. He wrote, "All things that are in the Father are beheld in the Son, and all things that are the Son's are the Father's. . . . Thus the Person of the Son becomes as it were the Form and Face of the knowledge of the Father, and the Person of the Father is known in the Form of the Son." God the Father is exactly like Jesus. What we see in Jesus is a full revelation of the nature of the Father. In Jesus we see *the form and face* of the Father. Therefore, we cannot see the Father as full of wrath and the Son as full of compassion. They are one and the same.

There are two wonderful Greek words that the early church theologians used to describe the Trinity: *kenōsis* and *perichōrēsis*. Kenosis is the act of self-giving for the good of another. It is found in the early Christian hymn in Philippians 2:

> [Jesus], though he was in the form of God,
>   did not regard equality with God
>   as something to be exploited,
>
> but emptied himself,
>   taking the form of a slave,
>   being born in human likeness. (vv. 6-7)

The word *emptied* translates the verb form of *kenōsis*. Jesus gave of himself for the good of another. The theologians reasoned that if Jesus was kenotic, the Father and the Spirit must be also. They used the word *perichōrēsis,* meaning "mutual submission," to explain it.

So the Father, the Son, and the Holy Spirit are living in mutual submission to one another. This is the heart of the Trinity: giving oneself for the good of the other. We like to think in terms of hierarchy, so we imagine the Father is the boss. The symbol used to explain it is a pyramid, with the Father at the top and the Son and Spirit at the bottom. But the kenotic and perichoretic nature of the Trinity abolishes hierarchy. As Dallas Willard said, "There is no hierarchy within the Trinity because the members of the Trinity will not stand for it." The better symbol for the Trinity is a circle.

So, what is the inner life of the Trinity like? Again, the word *perichōrēsis* gives us a clue. In addition to meaning "mutual submission," perichoresis also means "dynamic intermingling." Dr. Marty Folsom defines this aspect beautifully:

> There is union without loss of individual identity. When one weeps, the other tastes salt. It is only in the Triune relationship

of Father, Son and Spirit that personal relationship of this order exists, and the early church used the word "perichoresis" to describe it. The good news is that we have been included in this relationship and it is to be played out fully in each of us and in all creation.

The members of the Trinity are intermingling, known and fully known. Each of us is designed for and invited to participate in the greatest, truest, most real, most intimate relationship that exists: that of the Father and the Son. The Spirit reveals this to us and invites us to join. Wow.

*How can our understanding of these key words (*kenōsis *and* perichōrēsis*) impact our relationship with God?*

Reason and experience. Though the Trinity is beyond our comprehension, I believe it is best understood experientially. I have found my deepest connection to the reality of the Trinity through prayer. Paul describes my own experience:

> Likewise the Spirit helps us in our weakness; for we do not know how to pray as we ought, but that very Spirit intercedes with sighs too deep for words. And God, who searches the heart, knows what is the mind of the Spirit, because the Spirit intercedes for the saints according to the will of God. . . .
>
> Who is to condemn? It is Christ Jesus, who died, yes, who was raised, who is at the right hand of God, who indeed intercedes for us. (Romans 8:26-27, 34)

I have felt the Spirit pray through me, and I have felt Jesus pray for me. True prayer must be trinitarian: we pray *in the Spirit, through Jesus, to the Father.*

The richest times of prayer for me are when I ask the Spirit what I should pray about and pray for. The Spirit *searches my heart* and beckons me to love what God loves. They are always good, beautiful, and true things. They are for things like love, joy, peace, kindness—the fruit of the Spirit—either for myself or others.

Karl Rahner said that in practice most Christians are monotheistic; this was certainly true of my early Christian life. But now I am thoroughly trinitarian in practice. The Trinity is at the center of my life. I believe in the Trinity, not because the church has taught it but because I have experienced it.

IS IT BEAUTIFUL AND GOOD?

Having established the truth of the Trinity, can we say that it is beautiful and good? I find the Trinity the most beautiful and good thing in the world. Its beauty makes me say "wow," and its goodness makes me say "thanks." The late Celtic theologian John O'Donohue said it well:

> The Christian concept of god as Trinity is the most sublime articulation of otherness and intimacy, an eternal interflow of friendship. This perspective discloses the beautiful fulfillment of our immortal longing in the words of Jesus, who said, Behold, I call you friends. Jesus, as the son of God, is the first Other in the universe. . . . In friendship with him, we enter the tender beauty and affection of the Trinity. In the embrace of this eternal friendship, we dare to be free.

The Trinity—the beloved Community—is utterly beautiful and deeply good. The fact that we, who are made in God's image, are invited into the trinitarian community is the greatest invitation we could ever receive.

The Rublev Trinity icon. I have spent hours gazing at the famous icon of the Trinity by Rublev. It is a depiction of the scene in Genesis 18, where Abraham and Sarah are visited by three angels. Sarah prepares a meal for them while they sit at a table. In Rublev's icon, the three angels represent the Father, the Son, and the Holy Spirit. Like all icons, it is full of symbolism. The Father wears a gold robe, the color of perfection, the Source of all things; the Son wears a blue robe, the color of sea and sky, the place of human beings; the Spirit wears a green robe, the color of life, fertility, and growth. (Please google the Rublev Trinity to see it in color.) Each head nods in deference to the other, depicting perichoresis and kenosis. Each holds a staff of equal length, showing equality. Jesus, in the center, holds out two fingers, representing his humanity and divinity. There is a tree in the background, foreshadowing the wood of the cross.

Though I have been looking at the icon for years, only recently I discovered a possible answer to something that had never made sense to me. At the front of the table is a rectangular hole, and I always wondered what it meant. (Nothing in an icon is random; everything is symbolic.) Art historians have discovered glue residue in that rectangle. One

Rublev Trinity icon

explanation is that Rublev may have glued a mirror on the front of the table. While we do not know for sure (and we know this is uncommon), I find that possibility fascinating. If it is true, then a person standing before the icon would see their own face at the table. Even if it's not true, it gets to the heart of what the Trinity desires: for us to enter into their fellowship.

One other note about the Rublev icon. When I first saw the icon I thought the angelic figures were females, but upon closer inspection they are androgynous, neither masculine nor feminine. I think this is important because the language we use for the Trinity is male. *Father* and *Son* are male terms. While it is true that Jesus became a man, and spoke of God as "Father," the Godhead is neither male nor female. There is a great deal of feminine imagery of God in the Bible. In Deuteronomy 32:11, God is compared to a mother eagle who provides for and protects her young. In fact, the Hebrew word for Spirit (*rûaḥ*) is feminine. Theologian Simon Chan says of the Holy Spirit, we can imagine "her as Mama, as the one who conceives divine life in us and like a loving mother nurtures us to the fullness of risen life in Christ." While our language about God is masculine, I think it's wise to include the feminine side of the Trinity as well.

Whether or not there was an actual mirror in the icon, how do you react to the idea that the Trinity is inviting you to come to the table?

Including feminine imagery can expand the reach of the magnificent story. Consider Japan, for example, where Christianity has not been well received. Less than one percent of the population is Christian. One theory is the emphasis on a stern Father, as is portrayed in the shaming gospel, is off-putting in their male-dominated culture. The Japanese have a traditional saying that the four most dreadful things on earth are "fires, earthquakes, thunder-bolts, and *fathers*." The father, in Japan, is supposed to be (and most are) strict, authoritarian, and judgmental, while the mother is suffering, nurturing, and caregiving. As a result, the Japanese—especially men—revere their mothers. The Japanese writer Shusaku Endo is the only Christian author to successfully reach his people; he has done so by emphasizing the maternal image of God. Perhaps telling the magnificent story in the right way might reach those who have rejected the Western idea of an angry Father.

WHAT ELSE IS AT STAKE?

Earlier I stated that the Trinity has been missing in our churches and in our lives. What is at stake in not understanding and not inter-acting with the Trinity? The answers are too many to name, but I will address the main one: disconnection from God. In the shaming story I have no connection to Jesus or to God. I need Jesus for his blood but not his life, not his friendship. God the Father is angry; the Son appeased the Father's wrath and then ascended. The Spirit is not in the story at all. We remain disconnected. Forgiven, but disconnected.

I agree with Richard Rohr who wrote, "The greatest dis-ease facing humanity right now is our profound and painful sense of disconnection." Understanding the Trinity properly informs us that God wants a relationship with us, to be in fellowship with us, to commune with us in love and intimacy. It tells us God is not a distant, angry judge watching from a distance. It allows us to enter the circle and let God into every area of our lives, both the joys and sorrows, the pleasure and the pain.

What is at stake?

Awe.

Wonder.

Joy.

THE GOOD NEWS IS . . .

God is just like Jesus. And Jesus is beautiful, good, and true.

My friend and colleague Keas Keasler, who teaches a class on spiritual formation, recently asked the class to close their eyes and picture God. After a few moments he had them open their eyes and, if comfortable, share what they saw. Most of them said the same thing: "An old man with a white beard floating in the clouds, looking down at us." Keas then said, "If what you imagine God to be like is anything other than Jesus, then you have the wrong image of God."

Jesus is beautiful, and so are the Father and the Spirit: "The Word was made flesh, and dwelt among us, (and we beheld his glory, the glory as of the only begotten of the Father,) full of grace and truth" (John 1:14 KJV).

Jesus is good, and so are the Father and the Spirit: "God anointed Jesus of Nazareth with the Holy Ghost and with power: who went about doing good, and healing all that were oppressed of the devil; for God was with him" (Acts 10:38 KJV).

Jesus is true, and so are the Father and the Spirit: Jesus said to Thomas, "I am the way, and the truth, and the life. No one comes to the Father except through me" (John 14:6). "When the Advocate comes, whom I will send to you from the Father, the Spirit of truth who comes from the Father, he will testify on my behalf" (John 15:26).

The Trinity is beautiful, good, and true, and so is the magnificent story they tell.

CONTINUE OBSERVING, AND IF POSSIBLE, putting entries into your beauty, goodness, and truth journal. This week I would like you to focus on truth. Truth is always aligned with reality. You can count on the truth. Truth is that which works. The created world is full of truth—atoms and particles and chemicals. Gravity is true. Photosynthesis is true. A well-built home is true. Music contains truth. Math is full of truth. Two and two will always make four. You can count on it.

We also count on others to speak the truth to us. When we discover someone has lied to us, our relationship is fractured and trust is broken. This week, be conscious about your own speech. Try letting "your yes be yes and your no be no." In other words, say what you mean, and mean what you say. As always, speak the truth in love. I find this practice helpful: when I say something untrue, I repent of it on the spot. "I am sorry, but what I just said is not true. Here is the real truth." Far from having others get offended, I have had people thank me for telling the truth.

As with beauty and goodness, when you see it and write about it, make sure to give thanks to God for it. God designed us with the need for truth and to be true to ourselves. We were made to speak truth. That is truth incarnate. Look for people speaking truth. According to sociologists, our common discourse often contains more lies than we are aware of. Make an attempt to speak the truth in love as much as you can.

Bonus practice. For centuries many Catholic and Orthodox Christians have made the sign of the cross on their bodies. To some people this may seem odd at best and dangerous at worst. But the practice is not mere superstition. It is a symbolic act of recognizing the Trinity and your participation in it. As you move your hand from your forehead toward your belly you say, "In the name of the Father," and as you cross your heart you say, "and of the Son." This downward movement is symbolic of the kenotic descent of Jesus to be with us. Then you move your hand across your chest (left to right for Catholics, right to left for Orthodox; if you are neither, you make the call) and say, "and of the Holy Spirit." This sweeping across the chest symbolizes the horizontal movement of the Spirit in our hearts. The sign of the cross is a reminder of the trinitarian reality we live in. It is a way for our body to be honored as the temple of the Spirit.

BATHING IN BEAUTY

Wherever you turn your eyes,
the world can shine like transfiguration.
You don't have to bring a thing to it
except a little willingness to see.

MARILYNNE ROBINSON

NESTLED AGAINST THE SAN GABRIEL MOUNTAINS in Southern California is a former monastery that is now a retreat center called Mater Dolorosa. It is a beautiful place, filled with luxuriant gardens of trees and flowers flourishing along its hillsides. I spent two weeks there in the summer of 1997. The rooms are very small monastic cells, spartanly furnished with only a table, a bed, and a chair. I awoke one morning at six to have a time of prayer, Bible reading, and journaling before breakfast and class. I had just poured a cup of coffee and sat down at the desk when I felt an inexplicable urge to turn my chair to the window and gaze.

Just across a lush green lawn was a row of trees with pale yellow leaves. The sun was coming up, slowly illuminating them. *Okay*, I

thought to myself, *enough nature gazing. Time to get serious and pray.*
I closed my eyes and began to pray.

After a few moments I felt an inner nudge whispering, *Look!* I
glanced out the window to see the sunlight now dancing on the
trees. As the leaves quivered in a gentle breeze, their bright yellow
was now shining like gold. My soul began to glow as if it were lit
from within. I tried to say something, but the only word that
came out was "wow." For the next five minutes that's all I said:
"Wow. Wow. Wow."

Then the angle of the sunlight shifted and the leaves of gold
faded back to pale yellow. It was as if the Lord had passed by, as
he did with Moses, showing me only a glimpse of his glory
(Exodus 33:22-23). I felt transported. But it passed! I wanted it to
stay. And I wanted more.

I would later learn that these are two characteristics of beauty: it
never stays, and it never fully satisfies. But though I was disappointed
and unsatisfied, the encounter changed me. I had witnessed the
immense weight of the glory of God. C. S. Lewis captured what
happened to me in his essay "The Weight of Glory":

> We do not want merely to see beauty, though, God knows,
> even that is bounty enough. We want something else which
> can hardly be put into words—to be united with the beauty
> we see, to pass into it, to receive it into ourselves, to bathe in
> it, to become part of it.

That is exactly how I felt. I wanted to merge with the beauty that
made its way into my soul. I tried to write about this experience in
my journal, but words could not do justice to what had just happened to me. I knew only this: I felt I had been embraced by the
glory of God.

But what makes the world beautiful? Is there something in it
inherently beautiful, or is it merely a shimmering perception

formed in the eye of the beholder? Does beauty have anything to do with God—or the Christian life? Or is beauty a seductive temptress we must avoid (as many Christians have believed)?

WHAT DOES BEAUTY HAVE TO DO WITH GOD?

"Beauty has nothing to do with God or the Christian life—and it may lead us away from God." This narrative has been common among Christians. Beauty is

> *When have you encountered beauty in a surprising and soul-stirring way?*

very powerful. It strikes us at a deep emotional level. It can overwhelm us. And this makes us leery of it. Attractive things are alluring. God, many believe, wants us to avoid beauty lest we be seduced by it. For this reason, many Christians have viewed beauty as either irrelevant or dangerous. After the Reformation, many Protestants in Europe whitewashed their churches. Wanting to avoid the supposed idolatry of the Roman Church and its ornate buildings and statues, they banished all artwork. All that was left were white walls and perhaps a cross.

Beauty, they reasoned, did not lead to but rather away from God. Beautiful things will become idols. Some Protestants even banished musical instruments from the sanctuary, fearing that their sound would become the focus; only the human voice could be trusted to keep us focused on God. Artists and their art have often been suspect in the church. To be sure, the church also has a strong history with art. The glorious cathedrals, the paintings of Rembrandt, the sculpture of Michelangelo, Bach's *Mass in B Minor*, and Handel's *Messiah* are examples of art that glorifies God. But by and large, Christians are uneasy with beauty. The sensual is too close to the sinful.

No one ever taught me about the role of beauty in my spiritual life. It was not so much the danger of beauty but its neglect that characterized my life as a Christian. For me, Christianity was about dogma and doctrines, not desire and delight. The shaming story says nothing about creation or beauty. If it plays a role at all, it's in its first statement: "Realize you are a terrible sinner." Some of our sin is attraction to things we shouldn't be attracted to (a neighbor's house or spouse), which might lead us to think that beauty is inherently sinful.

In short, we have lost our love for beauty as a means to loving God—or, more accurately, to feeling the love of God.

IS IT BEAUTIFUL AND GOOD?

The narrative that beauty can be dangerous has some merit. Beauty can be seductive. As Dostoevsky said, "The awful thing is that beauty is mysterious as well as terrible. God and the devil are fighting there and the battlefield is the heart of man." We are attracted to beauty. The devil knows this. When beauty becomes the ultimate, it becomes an idol. But that is true of anything we make ultimate. Jesus criticized the Pharisees for making the law ultimate. Practically anything can become an idol if we make it ultimate. I once saw a bumper sticker that said, "Fishing is my life." My first thought was, *That guy can do better*. But my second thought was, *Sounds like idolatry*. A better bumper sticker would read: "Fishing: Thanks, God."

When we see beauty as either irrelevant or dangerous, we miss out on one of God's greatest gifts. God has given us five amazing senses. And each of them is designed to delight in beauty, goodness, and truth. Beauty is meant to lead us to God. Beauty is meant to move us to doxology. Beauty is never the ultimate. It is designed to be *penultimate*, to lead us to something beyond itself. If something is beautiful, it is good and true. A right understanding of beauty can enhance our lives on every level. Sensual beauty (a delicious meal, a starry night) and intellectual beauty (a mathematical equation, the idea of the Trinity, the teaching of Jesus) are designed to enhance our lives and deepen our love for God.

Recently, when I was in London, I went to the National Gallery. It was a weekday, but it was still crowded with people wearing headsets, staring at famous paintings, listening to a narrator explain the background and interesting aspects of the paintings. People walked about in a hushed reverence. Some had a look of awe and wonder on their faces. Then it hit me: art museums today are secular cathedrals. Modern culture has largely jettisoned God, but the longing for beauty cannot be removed from our souls. Tom Wolfe said in a lecture, "Today art . . . is the religion of the educated classes." It is a religion that asks nothing of the adherent, beyond the price of admission. It requires no surrender, submission, or service. It does not demand moral behavior or personal change.

> *Do you agree that the appreciation of art is a kind of religion for people today? What does this tell us about the power of beauty?*

We will always be drawn to beauty. In terms of drawing us to the heart of God, beauty is more powerful than truth or goodness. The true and the good meet with a resistance that does not hold for the beautiful. Beauty is nearly irresistible. "It is the prerogative and charm of beauty to win hearts," said Miguel de Cervantes. The question is: Will its charm lead us to God or be an end in itself, thus becoming an idol? God uses beauty to draw us, goodness to hold us, and truth to convince us.

WHAT SCRIPTURE SAYS ABOUT BEAUTY

It seems that the vast majority of Christians skip over the first two chapters of the Bible (Genesis 1–2, the story of creation) and begin with Genesis 3 (the story of the fall). In the same way, most Christians stop reading the Bible at Revelation 20 (the fiery pit of hell) and leave out Revelation 21–22 (the new heavens and the new earth). That is because the shaming story starts with our sin and ends with our final judgment. But the first two and the last two chapters of the Bible are essential. God created the heavens and the earth out of joy and for our benefit. And despite our rebellion and destructive ways, God is on a mission to rescue us and to create a new heaven and a new earth in his final act. But that is getting ahead of the story.

The magnificent, true story begins this way: "In the beginning when God created the heavens and the earth" (Genesis 1:1). The Bible does not tell us how or why or when the world was created. It only tells us *who* created it: God. We then learn what God thinks of the world God has created: "God saw everything that he had made, and indeed, it was very good" (Genesis 1:31). Something is good because it benefits, enhances, heals, and enlivens. The natural world is full of goodness. This morning I ate an English muffin with honey and peanut butter, and washed it down with a cold glass of milk. It was good for me. It benefited me. But I also enjoyed it. God looked at creation and noted that it was good. God could have easily said, "Indeed, it is very beautiful."

The Bible does not use the word *beauty* very often, except to talk about human beauty (and how it fades). Instead, the preferred word is *glory*. Glory is beauty, goodness, and truth combined with power. The psalmist declares, "The heavens are telling the glory of God; and the firmament proclaims his handiwork" (Psalm 19:1). So when we gaze on a shining, silver moon, we are witnessing the glory of God. God made the moon and the sun, which provides the light the moon reflects, and each night they are telling the magnificent story.

The created world demonstrates the glory (power and beauty) of God. The apostle Paul stated it clearly: "Ever since the creation of the world his eternal power and divine nature, invisible though they are, have been understood and seen through the things he has made" (Romans 1:20). The created world is not lifeless, meaningless matter. In the rocks and the trees, the skies and the seas, the invisible power of God becomes visible. The glory of God shines through the beauty of creation.

The world is not merely beautiful, it is also good. It is a perfectly designed habitat for its inhabitants. When we read Genesis 1, instead of worrying about the wheres and whens and hows of creation, let's read it as a story of Someone building a home, a place for living things to dwell. In this sense, the created world is an act of *hospitality*. God tells Adam and Eve that he has built a great home for them:

> God said, "See, I have given you every plant yielding seed that is upon the face of all the earth, and every tree with seed in its fruit; you shall have them for food. And to every beast of the earth, and to every bird of the air, and to everything that creeps on the earth, everything that has the breath of life, I have given every green plant for food." And it was so. God saw everything that he had made, and indeed, it was very good. (Genesis 1:29-31)

Human beings are not necessary to the world; their invitation to thrive is an act of grace. The sun, the sky, the land and oceans, the fish and birds and cattle are utterly gratuitous—freely given acts of grace from a God whose first act in the story makes this clear statement: we are loved. The created world is good, and it is also *true*—that is, real. Mountains are very real. There is no deception in them. And the laws of the natural world are true. Gravity is not subjective. Reality is what you can count on, and the created world is completely reliable—at times dangerous, but always true.

GOD IS NOT SILENT

What are your thoughts and feelings when you reflect on the world as "a perfectly designed home"?

Many wonder why God is not more vocal. If God wanted to, God could appear at the foot of our bed each morning or write messages to us in the sky or shout to us through a divine bullhorn. Instead, God chooses to speak to us in noncoercive ways. God is speaking to us all the time through the beauty and complexity and diversity of the created world. Michael Kendrick describes this well:

> If God wanted to remain silent about His existence, He wouldn't have bothered creating the stars; He wouldn't have made the Milky Way, or Betelgeuse. In fact, He wouldn't have made the majestic Rocky Mountains, the rippling oceans, or the magnificent hummingbird. If His goal was to remain quiet and anonymous, He wouldn't have created anything at all.
>
> Instead, He spoke into existence a smorgasbord for our senses. Wonder for our eyes, beauty for our ears, fragrances for our noses—and rapture for our hearts. His creation screams about His unseen beauty; it shouts about His unseen qualities and His magnificence.
>
> When Michelangelo painted the ceiling of the Sistine Chapel, he crafted an outward expression of his inner person. In the same way, God's creation exhibited through the mountains, stars, and oceans is an expression of the God we can't see. . . .

God didn't remain anonymous because He didn't want to. Rather, He wanted to display His glory throughout the universe as His gift to man.

Creation silently shouts God's invisible beauty. This is why Paul said we are "without excuse" when it comes to knowing about God. God has revealed himself through creation: "Ever since the creation of the world his eternal power and divine nature, invisible though they are, have been understood and seen through the things he has made. So they are without excuse" (Romans 1:20).

WHAT TRADITION SAYS ABOUT BEAUTY

Several of the great theologians in the early church affirmed the importance of beauty. St. Augustine, writing in the fourth century, tells of a time he asked the created world why it exists:

> I asked the earth, I asked the sea and the deeps, among the living animals, the things that creep. I asked the winds that blow, I asked the heavens, the sun, the moon, the stars and to all things that stand at the doors of my flesh. My question was the gaze I turned to them. Their answer was their beauty.

Things exist, Augustine believed, because they are beautiful. And we naturally love that which is beautiful. Augustine said in his treatise on music, "Only the beautiful is loved, . . . we cannot help loving what is beautiful." Another early church theologian who was deeply focused on beauty was Dionysius the Areopagite. He wrote an entire book on beauty and goodness, saying, "And so it is that all things must desire, must yearn for, must love, the Beautiful and the Good."

The saints and theologians of the medieval church made much of the importance of beauty. Bernard of Clairvaux said, "Believe me, you will find more lessons in the woods than in books. Trees

and stones will teach you what you cannot learn from the masters."
The sixteenth-century Spanish mystic John of the Cross wrote
beautiful poetry about the power of beauty, such as this:

> I did not
> have to ask my heart what it wanted,
> because of all the desires I have ever known, just one did I
>   cling to
> for it was the essence of
> all desire:
> to hold beauty in
> my soul's
> arms.

The tradition of the church has always held the importance of
beauty in the Christian life.

One of my favorite writers is Simone Weil. She was raised
Jewish but was struck by the beauty of Jesus. She came to accept
the tenets of Christianity but was never baptized. She wrote many
essays and books but did not become famous until after her death.
In them she wrote the following about beauty: "The created world
is the sign of love between the Creator and creation." "God created
the universe and his Son . . . created the beauty of it for us."

My favorite image she offers is that in the created world we see
Christ's "tender smile for us coming through matter" and that the love we
have for it "proceeds from God dwelling in our souls and goes out to
God present in the universe."

Perhaps the most influential theologian who teaches the importance of
beauty is Hans Urs von Balthasar.

What is your reaction to Weil's statement that Jesus is smiling at us through the beauty of things?

Balthasar, writing in the late twentieth century, wrote a fifteen-volume treatise on beauty, goodness, and truth. He wrote, "A moment of grace lies in all beauty: it shows itself to me far beyond what I have a right to expect, which is why we feel astonishment and adoration." Altogether, the witness of the saints is consistent: beauty is an integral part of our life with God. It can seduce us if we make it an idol. But if we treat it as an icon—or as a sacrament—then beauty has the power to deepen our love for God. Beauty is a portal to God.

WHAT DO REASON AND EXPERIENCE TELL US ABOUT BEAUTY?

If we had only reason, and not faith, we could still arrive at this conclusion: we live in an enormously marvelous, vast, complex, intricate universe whose form is sheer beauty. Human beings are not required to love it, appreciate it, or give praise to God for it. This tells me, by reason, that the Creator is loving. Love gives but never demands. Of course, we ought to be giving thanks and praise constantly for the beauty, goodness, and truth of the created world. But God does not demand it. God longs for us to offer it freely.

I was not aware of the role of beauty for much of my Christian life. I was aware of and attracted to beauty, but I did not make the connection between beauty and God in my experience. That has drastically changed. As my friend Rich Mullins once wrote, "There's so much beauty around us, for just two eyes to see. But everywhere I go . . . I'm looking." My Christian life has shifted from my mind to my senses. I am learning to feel the love of God in a sunrise, to taste the love of God in a meal, and to be embraced by the love of God in a gentle breeze.

As I write, I am watching Nebraska's North Loup River gently flow and sparkle as it reflects the sunlight. My dog, Winston, is sleeping at my feet. I am listening to music by the brilliant composer

Ludovico Einaudi. Wild turkeys will be coming by to roost in the trees to the south of the cabin. Across the river the cows and their calves are anxiously mooing; this morning the farmer separated them for weaning. There is a pulsing energy around me I used to fail to see. Now I am moved to doxology, to praise God. A rhythm is going on around me. Like Simone Weil, I am learning to see Jesus' "tender smile for us coming through matter."

IS IT GOOD?

The created world is good and true, meaning that it is beneficial and useful. We can rub sticks together and make a spark that becomes a flame, which keeps us warm. Good and true, thus useful. But the world is also beautiful. It does not need to be beautiful to be useful. So why is it also beautiful? Two Latin words are used to describe useful and beautiful things: *util* and *frui*. *Util* means useful, beneficial, helpful. *Frui* means enjoyable, pleasurable, and delightful. The created world is both *frui* and *util* at the same time. The sun is *util*; a sunset is *frui*. We need the sun. If that big star went out, we would die. But we don't need sunsets to be *beautiful*. They just are. This part of the story tells us that the hospitable God who made us wants us not only to survive but to thrive.

We do not need beauty to live. But we need it to live well. God made us with an innate longing for more than survival. That something more is beauty. We distinguish between the *practical* arts—sciences such as architecture, carpentry, and engineering for producing useful structures such as homes, buildings, and bridges—and the *fine* arts—pursuits such as poetry, literature, musical composition, and performance.

We need the practical arts, but they can also be beautiful—pleasing to the senses. I was recently in Sydney, Australia, and got to see the famous Sydney Opera House. It serves a practical purpose as a place to gather for concerts and live events. But it is also beautiful to see, like an art exhibit. The fine arts are not "practical" in that they are materially necessary for physical survival, but they enhance human existence. Beauty is what gives depth to our lives in meaning and purpose. Beauty creates passion. Most importantly, beauty is the portal through which God reaches and woos us.

Rarely do we see a rainbow without experiencing awe. Even when we are feeling down or preoccupied, a rainbow captures our attention and evokes awe. Colors themselves evoke emotions. Red, for example, is an intense and passionate color. Green is the color of growth and brings feelings of hope. And violet is the royal color, associated with spirituality and wealth.

> *Which do you find more appealing, things that are useful or things that are beautiful?*

Like colors, musical notes also evoke emotions. In general, major keys usually relate to love, hope, and joy, while minor keys often relate to sadness or melancholy. Though we are not always consciously aware of it, sounds, like colors, create feelings in us.

Flavors too can impact us emotionally. The five major flavors are sweet, salty, sour, savory, and bitter. God designed us with a tongue that can detect each of these flavors. The taste of something can create an emotional response that we find difficult to put into words. My friend John Pavetto enjoys sharing with friends the wines he loves. One evening John handed me a glass of wine and I took a sip. It was delicious. John said, "This wine tastes like the first time you kiss the love of your life."

The point of all this talk about form and color, sound and taste, is that we seldom reflect on this simple fact: *it does not have to be*. The world does not have to be beautiful; we do not have to have ears and eyes tuned for such sensitivities; the color green is not necessary; and we have done nothing to merit the taste of chocolate. But they are all there. Our Host is an artist, an engineer, a chef, and a musician. Without any other divine revelation than what we can taste and see, we know this: we are loved. And love alone is credible, said Balthasar. "Everything that is—every tree, bird, star, stone and wave—existed first as a dream in the mind of the divine artist. Indeed, the world is the mirror of the divine imagination and to decipher the depths of the world is to gain deep insights into the heart of God." This ought to lead to a *hallelujah* every moment of our lives. The poet Gerard Manley Hopkins said it best: "Glory be to God for dappled things."

WHAT IS AT STAKE?

Failure to live with God through beauty has several negative consequences. First, it will make it difficult to pray and love. Balthasar said that whoever does not appreciate beauty "can no longer pray and soon will no longer be able to love." When we connect to God through beauty, praying and loving come naturally. We need to be alive to the awe and wonder we find in beauty. Albert Einstein once said, "He who can no longer pause to wonder and stand rapt in awe is as good as dead."

We also become bored, which Kierkegaard called the root of all evil. In our boredom we become tired. In his book *Beauty: The Invisible Embrace*, John O'Donohue wrote, "When we lose sight of beauty our struggle becomes tired and functional. When we expect and engage the Beautiful, a new fluency is set free within us and between us. The heart becomes rekindled and our lives brighten with unexpected courage." Many people would be surprised to know that the great philosopher Dallas Willard actually taught a class on art and aesthetics. Dallas knew the importance—rather, the necessity—of the transcendentals in the Christian life. In a chapel talk on the subject of salvation he said,

> If your salvation does not include living with God in beauty,
> truth, and goodness, it's going to be a very dry haul. And so
> much of our difficulty today for Christians in this world, and
> for the world without a vital Christianity in its midst—so
> much of the problem comes from having a Christ who has no
> association with beauty, maybe not even truth, not goodness.
> . . . A Christ without beauty, truth, and goodness is a testimony
> against the goodness of God, the grandeur of God.

When we think of salvation, we think of what happens after death.
For Dallas, salvation is deliverance from evil in all its varied forms.
Salvation must include living with God in beauty, goodness, and
truth. This is what we must learn to live into, and learn how to lead
others into as well.

I met a woman in Australia whose husband planted a new church
in Sydney. She leads a group of young women. She said to me,
"When I talk to them about living a beautiful life, they light up. This
is what is drawing them to God." In an age when truth and goodness
are met with so much resistance, perhaps only beauty can break
through those barriers and reach into our hungering hearts.

THE GOOD NEWS IS . . .

The Trinity is beautiful. We do not have to do anything to make
that so. Everything about Jesus is beautiful. Often I hear people say,
"We need to get people to commit to Jesus." My response is always
the same: "We need to get people to know Jesus." When they come
to know Jesus, they will be struck by his beauty. It will sneak past
defenses and speak to a generation suspicious of truth claims and
unconvinced by moral assertions. Brian Zahnd said it best: "Our
task is not to protest the world into a certain moral conformity, but
to attract the world to the saving beauty of Christ."

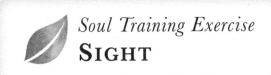

THIS WEEK WE ARE EXPANDING on our beauty journal by exploring how God woos us with beauty through the five senses. Each practice is meant to be creative and open, so you can make changes and do what you want, but I've offered suggestions if you are unsure what to do. With each practice, it is important to shift the focus from the beauty of what you are experiencing (the penultimate) to the Source of all beauty (the ultimate). This week we will focus on sight.

Sight exercise. Set aside time to simply see something beautiful. Before you begin, take a moment to pray and remind yourself that God is present and is also looking at this thing of beauty. Things you could do:

- watch the sunrise or the sunset
- observe a hawk swirling through the sky
- tour an art museum

Notice the details. Observe the colors, the form, the movement, the subtle nuances that make this object beautiful.

As you grow in awareness of this beautiful thing, turn your awareness into expressions of gratitude toward God. These might be words like *thank you, wow,* or *oh!* Or you might be speechless—that's okay, you can let the Spirit pray for you in a speechless moment.

Then, before you move on with the rest of your day, take a moment to remember that the beauty surrounding us is God's way of wooing us into a loving relationship.

EMBRACING OUR GOODNESS

The basic human drive is the desire for the Good.

JOHN O'DONOHUE

RICH MULLINS WAS A CHRISTIAN singer-songwriter who became famous in the late 1980s. He wrote hit songs for Amy Grant and eventually wrote and recorded hits for himself, such as "Awesome God" and "Step by Step." Rich came to Friends University, where I teach, as a student in 1991. We quickly became friends, and eventually he moved into our attic apartment where he lived with us for two years. Before he moved in, he came over late one night and wanted to talk. We usually joked around a lot, but on this evening his serious look gave me an eerie sensation. We walked upstairs to what would become his apartment and sat down. He got right to the point.

"I would like to be close friends with you, and if that is going to happen, you have to really know me," he said.

"Okay, well, I have known you for about a year, so I know you as . . ."

"No, you don't know me," he cut in. "You know I'm famous. You've heard my music. You know I'm from Indiana, went to Cincinnati Bible College, worked in Nashville, and left my career to teach music to Native American children on the reservation. You know all that stuff, but you don't know my sin and brokenness. If we're going to be friends, you need to know the depths of my depravity. This will make or break our friendship, but I'm willing to risk it because I want a friend, not a fan. Are you okay with this? It'll be hard to hear."

I was trembling. "Okay," I said. "Let it all out."

He walked me through years of mental and physical abuse, of sin and wantonness. It was a story of reckless, selfish, sinful behavior.

He was right. It was hard to hear. But not in the sense that I thought less of him. Oddly, it was kind of beautiful—raw and honest and real. He was not in any way proud of his behavior. He had a look of deep remorse. It was hard to hear because of all the pain that drove him to sin, and all the pain the sin had then inflicted on him.

I told him I still loved him, and that I appreciated his sharing his story with me. He seemed very appreciative. I assumed it was my turn. "Well, I guess I should air out my dirty laundry as well."

"Naw, you don't need to do that," he stopped me again (he did that a lot). "It will be boring after hearing mine. And besides, sin is pretty much the same for all of us. Let's leave it at this: we are both ragamuffins who need love and grace."

But he did have more he wanted to say. "The reason I wanted to confess is that you met me only after I became famous. And the truth is, after I became famous, everyone assumed that I was and had always been a perfect Christian. A lot of the sin I shared with you happened *after* I was famous. Try to work that one out!" he laughed.

Then it hit me. He had just exposed a part of the old narrative I was still holding on to: "God works only through the righteous."

The scary and shaming story insisted that the power of the message depended on the purity of the messenger. Now, I had a conundrum: Rich Mullins was a sinner. God used Rich Mullins. It was time I started to learn another part of the great story that has been going on forever: despite our sin, sin is not our identity.

The point of this chapter is this: sin is not our essence; it is a willful act of separation that mars our likeness to God. My friend Rich recounted steps of disobedience in which he was trying to replace his deep longing for relationship with God and others. We sin every time we turn from God, self, and others to seek solace in something that cannot deliver the promise it makes. Rich described this paradox beautifully in his song "Hold Me Jesus." He wrote the song when he was in Amsterdam. It was late in the night, and he was under a great deal of temptation. He wrote these words:

> *Have you ever had someone confess their sin and brokenness to you—or you to someone else? What did that feel like? Did you think less of them?*

> Surrender don't come natural to me.
> I'd rather fight you for something
> I don't really want
> Than to take what you give that I need.

Surrender is not natural to us. Sin seems like a way to meet our needs. So we fight God for something we ultimately do not want, rather than take what God wants to give, which is actually what we need. We struggle because we are made in God's image. We long for good, to be good, and to do good. When we find we are not and have not, all is not lost. We can discover what causes us to sin and why, as Rich found. And we find our freedom not in hiding our brokenness but in disclosing it.

THE DOMINANT NARRATIVE

Put simply, the dominant Christian narrative about our identity is this: "We are rotten sinners, we love to sin, and all we do is sin."

The shaming story begins with this point: "Realize you are a sinner." It is a shame-based, shame-driven story. It starts with the doctrine of original sin, which is the notion that Adam and Eve's first sin changed their fundamental nature: they and all of their offspring—everyone ever born—are born with a sinful nature. Adam and Eve broke the one and only commandment of not eating from the tree of the knowledge of good and evil. As a result they were banished from the Garden of Eden. Sin was now *in* them and would be passed on to their offspring for all eternity.

G. K. Chesterton once remarked that of all of the Christian doctrines, original sin was the most provable. After all, when we look at the world, or even into our own hearts, we see the evidence of sin. When we see—or feel—the depths of human depravity, it is easy to conclude that our very nature is sinful. St. Augustine was the first theologian to teach original sin in this manner. Augustine was a deeply carnal sinner before his conversion. In his biography, *Confessions*, he recounts seeing two babies being breastfed at the same time. One of the babies, Augustine claimed, looked at the other with envy. He uses this illustration to prove his doctrine that we are all born sinners, that our hearts are desperately wicked.

Augustine remains one of the most influential theologians in the church. His teaching on original sin formed the dominant narrative in the Western church. I am not rejecting the notion of original sin or that sin brought death and affects everyone. But there is more to the story of who we are, and more to the story of why we sin than "I was born that way. I can't help it. It is what I do." How we understand original sin is crucial.

IS IT BEAUTIFUL AND GOOD?

Is the narrative that we are born sinful beautiful? Beauty is that which pleases. It is hard to find anything pleasing about the notion that we are from birth rotten sinners. Beauty makes us say "wow." This narrative makes us say "woe." I believe we are all broken, weak, and capable of great evil. But it is not what we were made for or what we are made of. There is much more to us. There is a great deal of good in us. As you read this, someone somewhere is loving their neighbor, serving people in need, creating beautiful art, and speaking the truth in love. And that is beautiful.

Is it good? Goodness is that which benefits; it leads to wholeness. Goodness makes us say "thanks." This shaming narrative makes me say "thanks for nothing!" It tells me I was created as a complete sinner, that I was born this way. It is not our fault, but we are still responsible for it. It also implies that God is a lousy and unfair Creator. I see nothing good in it.

TRUE NARRATIVE

The true narrative says, "We are made in God's *image*, with original goodness, which cannot be marred by our sin. But we are also made in God's *likeness*, which we distort every time we choose to sin."

What the Bible teaches: image is everything. Is it true that we are rotten-to-the-core sinners? Is that what the Bible teaches? Is it supported by the tradition of the church? Does it make sense? Does it match with our experience?

The Bible says of humans, "God saw everything that he had made, and indeed, it was very good" (Genesis 1:31). This was said right after the last act of creation. The first thing we learn about humans is that we are good—*very* good. Instead of starting with original sin, we ought to start with our *original goodness*.

The Trinity is beautiful, good, and true. We are made in God's image. But Genesis 1:26 also says we are made in God's likeness: "Then God said, 'Let us make humankind in our image, according to our likeness.'" This means that we are—in our essence—beautiful, good, and true. That original image cannot be distorted or marred or vandalized by our sin. No matter how much Rich had sinned, he had never removed the image of God in him. But the early church taught that we, by our sin, *can distort our likeness to God.*

This is a fundamental point. Failure to understand this will lead to a host of problems. When I realize I am made in God's image, I understand I am sacred and valuable. When I understand that I cannot alter this image by my foolish, sinful ways, I am grateful to God. When I accept that by my actions I am either moving closer to or further from God's likeness, I take sin seriously. The shaming story does not say much about sin, other than it separates us from God. In truth, our sin separates us not only from God but from ourselves and others. It was not what we were designed for.

St. Paul writes, "We are God's handiwork, created in Christ Jesus to do good works, which God prepared in advance for us to do" (Ephesians 2:10 NIV). We are works of art in ourselves, but we are also called to participate in doing good works, in making our very life a work of art. We are created "to do good." This is the witness of the Bible.

Just as the singing of birds, the smell of flowers, and the colors of the rainbow touch our soul because we were made beautiful by God, so also when we experience goodness our souls are touched because we were made for goodness. We are designed to do and be good. Rich's failure to be good—which we all share—is an indication that sin is not right. That we are "good for nothing" is a false narrative. Our Creator created us to do good—that is our intended way of life.

A right reading of Romans 7. A passage often cited concerning our sinful nature is Romans 7. I once taught a Sunday school class on Romans. In Romans 7, a subject of controversy, Paul *appears* to be writing in the first person when he proclaims, "I do not understand my own actions. For I do not do what I want, but I do the very thing I hate" (v. 15). The day we looked at chapter 7, a woman began by saying, "Well, I feel better after reading this chapter." I asked her why. She said, "Well, if St. Paul struggled with sin, then that makes me feel better. Reading this chapter I felt like Paul had been reading my diary."

"But," I responded, "this chapter falls between chapter 6, where Paul proclaims our freedom from sin, and chapter 8, where Paul calls us to set our minds on the things of the Spirit, not the flesh—in other words, to walk in holiness."

"I don't care about chapters 6 and 8; I just like what he says in chapter 7. It makes me feel better about myself," she replied.

What she—and many others—failed to realize is that the "I" in Romans 7 is not Paul himself. I must point out that she is not alone: both Augustine and Luther agree with her. But modern scholars disagree. Luke Timothy Johnson is one of many scholars who believes that Paul is using a common rhetorical device called "speech in character." He is describing a character who is trying to keep the law in his own strength—and failing repeatedly. Paul knows the problem: the law can only *identify* sin but cannot *prevent* it.

The only value of the law is to reveal our sin. The law does not have the power to transform us; it is outside of us, judging us. Paul is trying to tell the Jewish Christians that they are no longer under the law. Christians are now "in the Spirit." We are "in Christ Jesus." Paul is not speaking autobiographically in Romans 7, nor is he depicting the Christian life. He is describing the futility of trying to establish a relationship with God by the law, which is impossible.

Finally, Romans 7 ends with a famous verse: "Wretched man that I am! Who will rescue me from this body of death?" (Romans 7:24). This verse is full of emotion and pain. A *wretched* person, we often think, is someone who is sinful and wicked. In the Greek, however, the word translated "wretched" is referring to misery. The person crying out is not confessing sin but is decrying their *miserable* life; the person is trying but getting nowhere. That is what happens when someone thinks they can find what they're looking for in the law and not in God's love and mercy.

What tradition says about our goodness. Augustine taught the doctrine of original sin. But as Karl Giberson notes, "Prior to Augustine, however, no such consensus existed and many Christians viewed Adam simply as Everyman, the first of our species, like us in many ways, tempted by Satan as we are." In fact the church fathers took the opposite side. Clement of Alexandria, writing in the second century, proclaimed, "When you see your brother, you see God." They emphasized that we are made in the image of God.

They also emphasized that we can and ought to grow in the likeness of God. The term they used for this process is *theosis*. Just as the Son has become like us in the incarnation, so also we can become like him by partaking in the divinity of the Holy Spirit. We can grow in our likeness to God. This is what Christian spiritual formation is aiming at. St. Athanasius, writing in the fourth century, wrote, "God made Himself man, that man might become God." This sentiment is also found in the writings of St. Gregory of Nazianzus and St. Gregory of Nyssa.

They taught that we are immediately endowed with the image of God, but we can acquire the likeness of God only by degree. St. John Chrysostom indicated that we come to resemble God as we develop the fruit of the Spirit in our lives. He also included truth, righteousness, humility, and the love of humanity.

We are sacraments of God's beauty, goodness, and truth. While some in church history have taught that humans are depraved sinners, it is important to know that has not always been the case. And throughout church history there has been teaching to the contrary. In the twentieth century, C. S. Lewis said, "There are no *ordinary* people. You have never talked to a mere mortal. . . . Next to the Blessed Sacrament itself, your neighbour is the holiest object presented to your senses."

What reason and experience teach about goodness. Finally, it is illogical to say that sin is normative when in reality it is always detrimental to us. It does not stand to reason. No one has ever sinned and been glad for its effect. That is because it is not what we were designed for. We were made good and made for good. That is an undeniable reality. Rich Mullins knew he had sinned and that his sin was wrong. He knew it harmed him. So the big question remains: If we were made good and to do good, why is there so much sin? One of my students, Jenna, asked this searching question one day in class: "Why is it that I, a person who loves Jesus so much, can sin so easily and so often?" The class fell silent for a moment at the gravity and honesty of her question. It is a great question. If it is not what we were designed for and is not our nature, then why do we sin?

WHY WE SIN

My colleague Stan Harstine has a helpful way of putting the issue: "Faith is the opposite of sin." So sin finds its origin in a *lack* of faith. Adam and Eve's sin was not trusting God. The temptation of the serpent went this way:

Now the serpent was more crafty than any other wild animal that the Lord God had made. He said to the woman, "Did

God say, 'You shall not eat from any tree in the garden'?" The woman said to the serpent, "We may eat of the fruit of the trees in the garden; but God said, 'You shall not eat of the fruit of the tree that is in the middle of the garden, nor shall you touch it, or you shall die.'" But the serpent said to the woman, "You will not die; for God knows that when you eat of it your eyes will be opened, and you will be like God, knowing good and evil." (Genesis 3:1-5)

The crafty serpent cast doubt in Eve's mind: "Can I trust God? Has God been lying to me?" The moment of doubt opens the door to sin.

Michael Polanyi brilliantly points out that we cannot *doubt* something without simultaneously *trusting* in something else. Eve began to doubt God—more importantly her relationship with God—at the same moment she began to trust the serpent. Christian psychiatrist Curt Thompson notes, "We are invariably made for faith, to operate out of a need to trust something we cannot control." As much as we do not like to admit it, we are *dependent* creatures. God is good and reliable, but we have the ability to doubt that. When we do, we look to put our trust elsewhere, in something we believe is reliable. When we doubt God's way is good or that God is out for our good, we turn to what we can control: a bottle, a pill, ice cream, lust, anger, gossip. And for a moment, we feel better. Until we don't—because those things are too small to feed the deep hunger of our souls.

I find myself in this dilemma each day. My hungering soul is easily misled into thinking sin will fulfill me. One week I set out to live without saying a negative thing about anyone. I was surprised at how often I started to do so and had to restrain myself. What I learned in this exercise surprised me. I felt more alive. It was as if I were living from a higher frequency. On the few occasions I failed,

I felt miserable. What I thought might feel good felt bad. It was another clear reminder that while sin is tempting, it is not what I was made for. Every time I chose not to do it, I was trusting in God, and that trust allowed me to interact with goodness, beauty, and truth. *That* is what I am made for.

The serpent had a clear intent in posing a question to Eve. It was not to seek an answer but to destroy relationships: between God and people, between the man and the woman. Doubt is a weapon of mass destruction for relational connection. If we doubt our spouse is faithful, or our boss has our best interest at heart, or our friend is truly reliable, the relationship is in jeopardy. And relational connection is our most important need. We can be talented and intelligent, but if we have no deep relationships we are lost. Our bank account can be massive and our waistline tiny, but if we do not have meaningful relationships in which we are known and loved, we have nothing. The key to relational connection? Trust.

When we fail to trust God, we create something in its place. According to Ray Anderson, in the story of the fall, "In deciding to eat the forbidden fruit, a decision against the self-authenticating Word is made in favor of the universal principle which holds that the good, the true, and the beautiful can be established independently of one's experience of the divine Word." That universal principle—the belief that we can create our own good, truth, and beauty apart from God—is the original (and never-ending) sin.

Thus, all sin is a form of idolatry. We put our trust in something other than God. It is difficult to admit that we are "empty, powerless, dependent, contingent beings." But instead of this making us feel ashamed, it ought to make us feel loved. We bring nothing to the relationship; God brings everything. I believe that is why Jesus tells us to become like children. Children are powerless and contingent and helpless beings—and they are not ashamed. In fact, they are *presumptuous*. They presume they will be cared for. We are ashamed of our helplessness. Shame prevents us from being known. We have to hide, and in hiding we will forever seek solace in something other than God (thus, making an idol) and be forever unhappy. Adam and Eve's fig leaves represent our attempt to hide.

THE PURSUIT OF THE GOOD

Despite our own sinfulness, brokenness, and proneness to wander from the throne of God, we have a deep need for goodness: not only to see the good but to be good. If someone were to say to us, "You know, I just don't think you have been very successful in your life," that would hurt most of us. But if someone were to say, "You know, I just don't think you are a *good* person," it would shatter most of us. That is because we are so committed to being good people—at least having others think we are—even if we do not live up to it.

I had a student assistant who was also a ballerina. She asked if I would watch her performance one evening, and I agreed. So I took my daughter Hope. On the way to the performance we made a quick stop for ice cream, which I had promised her. This made us ten minutes late. When we got to the auditorium, we went straight to the door, bypassing the box office, and went in between performances. The next week a student came to my office and said, "I just want you to know that I respected you as a man of God, but I no longer do."

"What happened that changed your perspective of me?" I asked.

"I saw you go into the auditorium without a ticket, as if you were above having to buy a ticket," he replied.

"Well, you can view my actions as you will, but in truth what I was doing was an act of kindness. First, I took my daughter for ice cream, but that made us late. Second, I was supporting one of my students in the ballet. The reason I did not get a ticket is because faculty get two free tickets for each performance. I already had my ticket."

His face fell. "I am sorry, I did not know all this."

But what hit me the most was how utterly hurt I was at first. When he said he had lost all respect for me, it was a serious blow to my heart. We want to be good, long to be good, and are deeply saddened when we discover others do not think we are good. Even if they are misled.

I find this longing to be good is a beautiful part of us, and it moves me to praise and worship. I praise God for weaving the longing for good so deeply in us that we cannot escape it. Much of our inner pain comes from the realization that we are, in fact, *not* good. That is what Rich Mullins had dealt with, and what he wanted to make clear in our friendship. He had not been good. He was not the person he assumed I thought he was because of his ability to write godly music that drew people to God's love. Rich was not afraid of the paradox of his own sinfulness and his longing to be good, to see good, and to do good.

> *It is painful when our actions or intentions are misunderstood, and someone mistrusts our good news. When have you longed for someone to see your goodness?*

He was broken, but he was also deeply good. One Christmas when he lived with us, he bought Meghan and me meaningful, thoughtful (and rather expensive) gifts. We bought him a CD. The imbalance in the gifts did not bother him in the least. He was so grateful for the CD. But more than that, he was happy to see how much we loved our gifts. He lit up when he saw how happy we were. After our daughter Madeline was born with severe birth defects, Rich called me. It was a strange conversation because Rich uncharacteristically said almost nothing. I later learned he was silent because he hurt for all of us and was so devastated by the news that he was speechless. A few months after that phone call he came to our house, unannounced, with his band. They played a song that he had written called "Madeline's Song." It moved us to tears and has been a blessing to us over the years. That same person who shared his deepest sins also shared with us his deepest goodness.

WHAT IS AT STAKE?

In addition to how we see ourselves, seeing others as sacred as opposed to sinful will impact how we relate to one another. If we see others as worthless, we will treat them with disregard and disrespect. If we see them as persons of great worth, we will treat them with dignity and due respect. We can then learn to draw out the good we find in others. My colleague Dona never fails to lift my spirits. She never fails to point out the good in me. As a result, I find myself longing to be better. A bumper sticker said, "Lord, help me to be the kind of person my dog thinks I am." I smile as I think of how Winston, on my best or worst day, looks at me with complete confidence.

Thinking of human beings as sinful and evil may help explain the sin and evil we see. It may also help us explain away our own sinfulness. But there is a great danger in this. It makes God responsible by proxy for all sin through the creation of flawed beings who constantly sin. And it prevents us from understanding why we sin. We sin when we mistrust God. We sin because we lose trust. Once we understand how that works, we can overcome it. Not that we will ever be free from sin, but sin is not like gravity. We are not under its dominion (Romans 6:12-14). Rather than being resigned to sin, I prefer to take ownership for my sin and to work on it. As Michel Quoist noted, "We are not God. We are simply the image of God and our task is gradually to discover that image and set it free."

THE GOOD NEWS IS . . .

We don't need to hide.

Because shame forces us to hide, the solution is to take the risk of being known as we are. I did not understand it at the time, but my friend Rich was modeling something important in his confession. At first I thought he just wanted to get something off his chest so he could get right with God. The shaming story had convinced me that we need to confess in order to get God to erase sin from the ledger. But Rich had moved well beyond the notion of God's ledger. He had come to know about the reckless, raging love of God. Rich had something else in mind: relationship.

When Rich laid bare his sins and transgressions, he was strengthening our relationship by allowing himself to be known. Sure, I could have rejected him. But he knew that would be better than not being known and therefore not being able to have a real relationship. Rich showed me that "evil is counting on us to hide." When we know and are known by God, sin becomes unnecessary. "Now, however, that you have come to know God, or rather to be known by God, how can you turn back again to the weak and beggarly elemental spirits? How can you want to be enslaved to them again?" (Galatians 4:9).

How do you feel about being known by God? Why?

In knowing and being known, we have what we need. We are becoming free.

In the last few years of Rich's life, I saw a drastic change in his character. I believe it was a part of his willingness to be known, to overcome shame, and to embrace the love of God. The rough edges became smoother, and the tendency to wander from God became less and less. He became a real model for the young men in his band. The real reason for this change was because he had grown close to Jesus. But that is getting ahead of our story. For now we need to turn to the beauty, goodness, and truth of a new and glorious covenant, and the part of the story that shocked the world.

Soul Training Exercise
SOUND

THIS WEEK WE ARE EXPANDING on our beauty journal by exploring how God woos us with beauty through the five senses. Each practice is meant to be creative and open, so you can make changes and do what you want, but I've offered suggestions if you are unsure what to do. With each practice, it is important to shift the focus from the beauty of what you are experiencing (the penultimate) to the Source of all beauty (the ultimate). This week we will focus on sound.

Sound exercise. For the sound exercise, we'll listen to something beautiful. Before you begin, take a moment to pray and remind yourself that God is present with you, listening to what you are listening to. You might even imagine Jesus sitting in the room with you. Then enjoy whatever music you find most beautiful. Perhaps it is a recording of Samuel Barber's *Adagio for Strings*, or Ella Fitzgerald singing "Take the 'A' Train," or a piece by Rachmaninoff. Whatever speaks to you.

If possible, find a place where you won't be interrupted or distracted. Maybe you could even turn out the lights and notice the sound and nothing else. You may want to dissect the sound—why do you love Fitzgerald's voice? Or perhaps you could not think about it but simply be surrounded by the beauty of the sound.

As the music ends, remember that God has surrounded us with beauty to draw us closer. End your time with words of gratitude to God, the giver of all beauty.

DISCOVERING THE TRUTH

And the Word became flesh and lived among us,
and we have seen his glory, the glory as of a
father's only son, full of grace and truth.

JOHN 1:14

S OMETIMES WE DISCOVER theologians in unexpected places. For me, it was in the comedy film *Talladega Nights*, starring Will Ferrell and John C. Reilly. They play NASCAR drivers Ricky Bobby and Cal Naughton Jr., who are best friends. One evening, they have a meal with Ricky's wife, Carley, his sons, and his father-in-law. Ricky decides to say grace. He prays,

> RICKY: Dear Lord Baby Jesus, or as our brothers in the South call you, Jésus. We thank you so much for this bountiful harvest of Dominos, KFC, and the always delicious Taco Bell. ... Dear Tiny Infant Jesus ...

> CARLEY: (*interrupting*) Hey, um, you know, Sweetie, Jesus did grow up. You don't always have to call him Baby. It's a bit odd and off puttin' to pray to a baby.

RICKY: Well, look, I like the Christmas Jesus best when I'm sayin' grace. When you say grace, you can say it to Grown-up Jesus, or Teenage Jesus, or Bearded Jesus, or whoever you want. . . .

(*more interruptions*)

RICKY: Dear Tiny Jesus, in your golden fleece diapers with your tiny, little, fat, balled-up fists. . . .

CAL: I like to picture Jesus in a tuxedo T-shirt, 'cause it says, like, "I want to be formal, but I'm here to party, too." I like to party, so I like my Jesus to party. . . .

RICKY: Dear Eight Pound, Six Ounce, Newborn Infant Jesus, don't even know a word yet, just a little infant, so cuddly, but still omnipotent. . . . Dear Baby God, Amen.

Ricky proclaims, "I like the Christmas Jesus best." Cal states, "I like my Jesus to party." Though a comedy and a spoof, the dialogue reveals a truth: we have the freedom to make Jesus to be whatever we want him to be, to tell the story that we have been told, or the story we want to tell.

Like Ricky, we want Jesus to make us feel most comfortable. Baby Jesus is sweet. Others like Jesus "the great Teacher." Still others prefer Jesus as "the Lamb of God," who takes away their sins. We like to control Jesus because it lets us control the narrative. We find the Jesus who makes us feel safe.

Jesus is good, but he isn't safe. Jesus is not tame. He is the Lion of Judah (Hosea 5:14; Revelation 5:5). The incarnation—the Son of God becoming human—is a *mystery*. It is beyond our understanding and beyond our control. It is also our only hope. Nevertheless, it is possible to twist and misinterpret the Bible to tell a story that is weak or even toxic. At the center of the great story is one key figure: God comes to us in the person of Jesus. And the revolution begins.

NARRATIVES THAT SHRINK JESUS

There are two narratives that shrink Jesus.

We need Jesus as only a teacher. The "good works" gospel sees Jesus primarily as a teacher. He can be compared to Socrates or the Buddha, an enlightened one. This was the view of my first pastor. He was a great teacher, but he was merely human. They are saying, "I like your teaching, Jesus. But I'm not interested in your miracles or even your death and resurrection. I only need your teaching."

We need Jesus for his blood only. The other dominant narrative about Jesus comes from the shaming gospel: "We only need Jesus for his blood." Jesus came only to die. This creates *vampire Christians*. They are saying, "Jesus, I only want a little of your blood, please."

Like Ricky Bobby, we can choose which Jesus we like: baby Jesus, teacher Jesus, or savior Jesus. But Jesus cannot be reduced to any one of them. Jesus said of himself, "I am the way, and the truth, and the life. No one comes to the Father except through me" (John 14:6). Jesus does

> *Why do we choose to make Jesus into what we want him to be, and not who he is in his fullness?*

not merely tell the truth, Jesus *is* the truth. The truth is always in sync with reality. The reality of Jesus is beyond anything we can ask or imagine. Our invitation into trinitarian life comes through Jesus, all of him, not merely the one aspect we find appealing.

THE TRUTH (AND GOODNESS AND BEAUTY) OF THE INCARNATION

The first disciples didn't fully grasp the reality and truth of who Jesus was. After his resurrection, Jesus appeared to them, and little by little they began to grasp the meaning of the incarnation. Paul's letter to the Philippians contains a passage that is either an early

Christian hymn or a part of the liturgy early Christians spoke while together. It is a beautiful description of the movement from the preexistent, preeminent Son of God to the man called Jesus:

> who, though he was in the form of God,
> 　　did not regard equality with God
> 　　as something to be exploited,
> but emptied himself,
> 　　taking the form of a slave,
> 　　being born in human likeness. (Philippians 2:6-7)

God left his divine throne to become a human being. He emptied himself, it says, to take on human form. The Greek word for "emptied" in this verse is *kenosis*. It means to sacrifice oneself for the good of others.

The one who created and sustains human beings has become a human being. C. S. Lewis aptly describes this miracle:

> The Christian story is precisely the story of one grand miracle, the Christian assertion being that what is beyond all space and time, which is uncreated, eternal, came into Nature, into human nature, descended into His own universe, and rose again, bringing Nature up with Him. It is precisely one great miracle.

The whole story is, as he said, "one great miracle." And it begins with the incarnation.

The prophet Isaiah foretold, "The Lord himself will give you a sign. Look, the young woman is with child and shall bear a son, and shall name him Immanuel" (Isaiah 7:14). *Immanuel* means "God *with* us." The Immanuel principle is *the* principle of the magnificent story. God was *with* Adam and Eve (until they rebelled). God was *with* Abraham. God was *with* Moses, and Esther and David and Elijah. But now, in Jesus, God is with *all* humanity in a new and special way. God is not just with an individual, a tribe, or a nation. God has come to establish a new *with-God life*, called the kingdom of God. And Jesus is the King.

But for now let's stay for a moment in the manger (Ricky Bobby would like that). Mary, with Joseph at her side, gives birth to an infant boy, in the most humble conditions—something akin to a barn. We must be careful not to sentimentalize the nativity story. Andrew Peterson captures the reality of the birth in his song "Labor of Love":

> It was not a silent night
> There was blood on the ground
> You could hear a woman cry
> In the alleyways that night
> On the streets of David's town
>
> And the stable was not clean
> And the cobblestones were cold
> And little Mary full of grace
> With the tears upon her face
> Had no mother's hand to hold
>
> It was a labor of pain
> It was a cold sky above
> But for the girl on the ground in the dark
> With every beat of her beautiful heart
> It was a labor of love

The King of kings and Lord of lords enters the world like any infant—weak, needy, and fragile. In "Welcome to Our World," Chris Rice sings of the wonder of *who* has entered our world:

> Fragile finger sent to heal us
> Tender brow prepared for thorn
> Tiny heart whose blood will save us
> Unto us is born

When we describe something so grand as God becoming human, our prose is too weak. We need poets like Peterson and Rice to help us grasp this wonder of wonders. The miracle of the incarnation is the centerpiece of the magnificent story. It is a love story, after all, and the hero is on the scene.

The incarnation is a statement of unconditional love. In the incarnation we experience the solidarity of God with humanity. God could have used countless ways to save us. Instead, he chose to enter our world and, as C. S. Lewis wrote, die and rise again, "bringing Nature up with Him." The incarnation is a proclamation of the value of humans. Permit me one more song. Of all the Christmas songs my favorite line comes from "O Holy Night": "Till He appeared and the soul felt its worth." The appearance of Jesus was an affirmation of our value and worth. God is on a rescue mission because we are somehow worth saving.

> *How does Jesus'*
> *appearance make our*
> *soul feel its worth?*

Only a beautiful, good, and true story is worth stepping into. The incarnation is all three. The *kenotic* act of becoming human to save us is the epitome of goodness. The countless changed lives indicate that it is indeed true. But it is also beautiful. The great bishop Bernard of Clairvaux described the beauty of the incarnation:

> How beautiful you appear to the angels, Lord Jesus, in the form of God, eternal, begotten before the daystar amid the splendours of heaven, "the radiant light of God's glory and the perfect copy of his nature," the unchanging and untarnished brightness of eternal life? How beautiful you are to me, my Lord, even in the very discarding of your beauty!

Bernard points out that in the act of self-emptying, Jesus actually becomes *more beautiful*. In the incarnation God's love shines and the sweep of grace widens. The Creator and Sustainer of the world now stands with us. Perhaps Chris Rice's lyrics work both ways. In the incarnation, Jesus says, "Welcome to *my* world."

MAGNIFICAT: THE MIGHTY REVERSAL

In the Gospel of Luke we find the songs of Elizabeth, Mary, Zechariah, and Simeon. These four explain Jesus' coming not in prose but in poetry. As New Testament scholar Norval Geldenhuys notes, Luke has collected these "stories which reveal the fact that when Jesus came into the world poetry expressed itself and music was reborn." The first song is from Mary's relative Elizabeth, singing of the blessed Mary who is bearing the Savior. The third is from Elizabeth's husband, Zechariah, who sings of how God is once again on the move, saving Israel through Jesus, and through Zechariah's own son, John the Baptist, who will pave the way.

The last hymn is sung by Simeon. He was a devout, elderly man who God promised would live long enough to see the Messiah. His brief hymn uses the image of a slave who has been instructed to watch through the long, dark night for the appearing of a special star, and to announce it when it appears. Led by the Spirit, Simeon enters the temple, where Mary and Joseph have come to present Jesus. With baby Jesus in his arms, he declares that God's salvation is now here, and that he can depart in peace because God, in Jesus, will save the whole world—including Gentiles (Luke 2:32). The light of truth will enlighten *every* person, Simeon declares.

The most famous of the four songs is Mary's (Luke 1:46-55). It is called "The Magnificat" because of her opening declaration that her soul *magnifies* the Lord. Her song is a lyrical poem comprising Old Testament quotations. The central message of her song is the *mighty reversal* God has always enacted but will do so more fully in Jesus. God reverses the typical human order. This world values power and might, rulers and thrones, wealth and possessions. God values humility, obedience, and mercy. The proud will be humbled; the poor will be filled. These four are singing about the truth. And in the birth, life, teachings, and actions of Jesus, we see this truth on display. From the very beginning, Jesus was starting a revolution.

The first, Jesus said, will be last. Those who lose their life will find it. Life works in a certain way. You can count on something only if it is true. Everything Jesus said and did is reliable because it is true. It actually *is* better to give than to receive. When we give we are operating at a higher kingdom frequency than when we receive. It is wonderful to receive, but even better to give. Jesus was, and is, a revolutionary—the most revolutionary revolutionist—not only in his day but to the present moment. That is because he was telling and living the truth.

JESUS: CREATOR, REDEEMER, SUSTAINER

Jesus' followers discovered that he was more than a preacher, a healer, and a redeemer. He was also *the Creator and Sustainer of everything*. In one of the most magnificent passages in the New Testament, Paul says about Jesus,

> He is the image of the invisible God, the firstborn of all creation; for in him all things in heaven and on earth were created, things visible and invisible, whether thrones or dominions or rulers or powers—*all things have been created through him and for him. He himself is before all things, and in him all things hold together.* He is the head of the body, the church; he is the beginning, the firstborn from the dead, so that he might come to have *first place in everything.*" (Colossians 1:15-18, italics added)

The story just added a massive new detail! The man we know as Jesus, the Teacher and Healer, is also the Creator.

Jesus created this world and continues to sustain it every moment. Jesus is holding the six trillion cells in my body together. He is sustaining thousands of galaxies. Jesus created and is supporting the gorgeous mimosa tree in my neighbor's backyard. He created and sustains the doves sitting on their eggs. He handles the sunlight that warms them all. This is not the belief that God is *in* all created things. God is not the sunlight, but God made it and sustains it.

Jesus is at the center of it all: "all things have been created *through* him and *for* him." Jesus made you, and you were made *for Jesus*. Things are beautiful not because we *deem* them so but because Jesus has *made* them so. The gospel message—the big story—must include this mind-blowing detail. The shrunken gospels start with me. But now we see that even before I'm in the picture, *Jesus is the center of all things*. The shrunken stories do not include this central truth: Jesus made it all. We sing, "Jesus paid it all." He did. But he also *made it all*.

Why is this an important part of the story? It is more than important; it changes the story entirely. Jesus is not just a great teacher. He's not only a sacrificial lamb. Jesus is the one through whom all things came into being, and without him not one thing came into being. Now his teaching and his sacrifice take on a whole new meaning. If Jesus were just a man, or even a man with special powers, he could not "make all things new." He might be wise, he might be able to heal, and he might be able to walk on water, but

> *How do you react to the notion that Jesus has created all things, that all things came through him and are for him?*

he cannot redeem the entire world—unless he is the Creator and Sustainer of everything.

ETERNAL LIFE NOW

This story's aim is not only to get people into heaven when they die or to make the world a better place. It is much bigger than that. God wants to draw us into the story so we can take part in eternal life now. Most Christians assume that eternal life begins when we die. Not according to Jesus. "And this is eternal life, that they may know you, the only true God, and Jesus Christ whom you have sent" (John 17:3). Eternal life is not merely unending life, it is a *quality of life*. It is *knowing* God and Jesus. Knowledge, in the Bible, is not merely intellectual, it is experiential.

The incarnation, God becoming human, created the possibility of relationship between God and humanity. God, in Jesus, entered humanity in order to draw us into divine life. The preeminent, preexistent, only begotten Son, who made all things, became a baby! Then a boy. Then a man. Then a rabbi. Then the Savior. Then the King. He did all of this so we could live in communion with God. In other words, so we could experience eternal life. Now.

John's first letter says:

> We declare to you what was from the beginning, what we have heard, what we have seen with our eyes, what we have looked at and touched with our hands, concerning the word of life—this life was revealed, and we have seen it and testify to it, and declare to you the eternal life that was with the Father and was revealed to us—we declare to you what we have seen and heard so that you also may have fellowship with us; and truly our fellowship is with the Father and with his Son Jesus Christ. We are writing these things so that our joy may be complete.

> This is the message we have heard from him and proclaim to
> you, that God is light and in him there is no darkness at all.
> (1 John 1:1-5)

This passage is powerful. The apostles saw, heard, and touched Jesus, and in so doing experienced eternal life, which is to know God the Father. In seeing, hearing, and touching Jesus they conclude with this one simple message: God is nothing but goodness and light. There is nothing bad about God.

This experience is not something earned but something God has done for us. Balthasar describes the divine descent:

> It is not our movement toward God, but God's movement to
> us. It is heaven interrupting our world . . . the descent of the
> divine light among human beings not only to shine on, to
> illuminate, to purify and to warm them, but, through grace,
> to make them also shine with a light not of this world.

God became human so humans could become like God. We are now able to be "participants of the divine nature" (2 Peter 1:4). Jesus emptied himself into human form so that we would one day glow.

JESUS' TRUTH WILL SET US FREE

One of the most commonly used and misunderstood sayings of Jesus is "the truth will make you free" (John 8:32). It is etched on countless university buildings. By themselves, those six words lead us to think that *truth* itself sets us free. But we can't interpret these words in isolation. They can only be understood in light of John 8:31. "Jesus said to the Jews who had believed in him, 'If you continue in my word, you are truly my disciples.'" Jesus is not saying that truth—as an abstract principle—will set us free but that truth is known by continuing in his word and by being his disciples.

Jesus was the greatest teacher who ever lived. His teachings are in line with reality, with truth. Jesus' teachings *work*. It truly is more blessed to give than to receive, to bless those who curse you, and to do unto others as you would have them do to you. The kingdom of God—Jesus' primary subject—really is like a mustard seed, leaven in dough, and a treasure hidden in a field. When we continue in his Word, and live as his disciples by living out his teaching, we find our lives aligning with reality. This is what it means to be set free by the truth.

> *Have you seen or heard those six words misused? How does placing those words in the larger context change their meaning?*

In one of my classes we studied Jesus' teaching about not letting "your left hand know what your right hand is doing" in relation to our acts of service (Matthew 6:3). One way I suggested to practice this is to engage in *secret service*, meaning, to do something nice for someone without them knowing who did it. One student, Austin, wrote in his reflection, "During this exercise I felt happy. I swept the floor in the house where my roommates and I live. I folded their laundry. I even cleaned the inside of one of their cars. I enjoyed getting to serve my roommates, to lighten their load. Through this exercise I learned that there is a great reward in serving others and not having to get credit for it." I loved his first statement: I felt happy. Austin was living out Jesus' teachings, and he was experiencing the reality that it actually is "more blessed to give than to receive" (Acts 20:35).

JESUS' WENT ABOUT DOING GOOD

Not only are his teachings true and reliable, but Jesus displayed *goodness* par excellence in his life and actions. His disciples noticed this. When Peter preached to Cornelius and his family in Acts 10, he said: "God anointed Jesus of Nazareth with the Holy Spirit and with power; [and] he went about doing good and healing all who were oppressed by the devil, for God was with him" (Acts 10:38). God the Father anointed Jesus with the Holy Spirit (a trinitarian event) and filled Jesus with power, which he used to do good. Good always benefits. Everyone *benefited* from their encounter with Jesus.

Jesus healed the sick and set the captives free, which he foretold in the synagogue talk:

> When he came to Nazareth, where he had been brought up, he went to the synagogue on the sabbath day, as was his custom. He stood up to read, and the scroll of the prophet Isaiah was given to him. He unrolled the scroll and found the place where it was written:
>
> "The Spirit of the Lord is upon me,
>   because he has anointed me
>   to bring good news to the poor.
> He has sent me to proclaim release to the captives
>   and recovery of sight to the blind,
>   to let the oppressed go free,
> to proclaim the year of the Lord's favor." (Luke 4:16-19)

After reading this passage, found in Isaiah 61:1-2, Jesus turned to the people listening and said, "Today this scripture has been fulfilled in your hearing" (Luke 4:21).

Jesus proclaimed the gospel (good news) and also lived and taught the gospel. The Sermon on the Mount and the parables proclaim the gospel, but so do Jesus' healings and interactions with people. When he stood with the woman caught in adultery, he was proclaiming good news. When he healed the Canaanite woman's daughter, he was demonstrating good news. Scot McKnight says, "The central question of the gospel is not how can I be saved, but who is Jesus? Your relationship to Jesus unleashes redemptive power. I hear people say, 'We need to get people to make a commitment to Jesus.' My response always is, 'We need to get people to *know* Jesus.'" If they come to know Jesus, in his beauty, goodness, and truth, they will naturally make a commitment to him.

We were designed for Jesus' pattern of life. As Mark McIntosh wrote, "Every human person is predisposed to discover the truth of reality by coming to share—practically, concretely, spiritually— in the life-pattern of Jesus." We can participate in, for example, his standing in solidarity with the woman caught in adultery. We can be immersed in that event. This is a part of what it means to be in Christ or to have Christ in us. Jesus lives by giving himself away.

JESUS AS THE NEW ADAM AND NEW ISRAEL

Jesus' restoration of the people of Israel is another good, beautiful, and true thing. God had made covenants—promises—with Israel: "I will be your God and you will be my people." The covenant failed, not because of God but because of the faithless, selfish, fearful, and rebellious people. Yet, out of his steadfast love, God kept pursuing the wayward people. God never gave up. In Jesus, God fulfills Israel's responsibility to the covenant. For example:

- Adam and Eve succumbed to the temptation of the serpent. But Jesus was tempted by and resisted the temptation of the serpent.

- The people of Israel wandered forty years in the desert and succumbed to temptation. Jesus fasted for forty days in the wilderness and resisted the temptation.

After Jesus' fast, he was baptized in the Jordan River, the river the Israelites crossed as they entered the Promised Land. Jesus restored Israel through his obedience. Paul refers to Jesus as the last, or new, Adam (1 Corinthians 15:45). He does not call him the second Abraham. The second Adam means that Jesus has brought redemption to all humans—Jews, Gentiles, and barbarians (Colossians 3:11).

Paul states his gospel succinctly: "Remember Jesus Christ, raised from the dead, a descendant of David—that is my gospel" (2 Timothy 2:8). Note there are only three parts to his gospel. First, Jesus is the Christ. *Christ* is the Greek word for "Messiah." The Messiah was the long-awaited Savior of Israel. Second, Jesus rose from the dead. In the resurrection of the Son, God defeats sin and death. Third, Jesus is a descendant of David. Jesus comes from a line of kings. He rescues the lost sheep of the house of Israel (and everyone else). A magnificent story! As N. T. Wright said, "Jesus is the resolution to a story in search of a completion."

> *What is helpful or encouraging to you about Paul's succinct explanation of the gospel?*

JESUS IS GOOD EVEN IF YOU THINK HE IS NOT

The people of Israel were promised the land of Canaan (Exodus 13:11), and they took hold of it with violence. The history between the Israelites and the Canaanites was one of discord, prejudice, and violence. So when Jesus took his disciples to the regions of Tyre and Sidon—the land of the Canaanites—it was a surprise (Matthew 15:21). In a puzzling story, Jesus is confronted by a Canaanite woman, and their conversation leads us to think that Jesus is being cruel:

Just then a Canaanite woman from that region came out and
started shouting, "Have mercy on me, Lord, Son of David;
my daughter is tormented by a demon." But he did not answer
her at all. And his disciples came and urged him, saying,
"Send her away, for she keeps shouting after us." He answered,
"I was sent only to the lost sheep of the house of Israel." But
she came and knelt before him, saying, "Lord, help me." He
answered, "It is not fair to take the children's food and throw
it to the dogs." She said, "Yes, Lord, yet even the dogs eat the
crumbs that fall from their masters' table." Then Jesus answered her, "Woman, great is your faith! Let it be done for
you as you wish." And her daughter was healed instantly.
(Matthew 15:22-28)

On the surface, it appears Jesus wants nothing to do with this
woman. Jesus took his disciples to a Gentile province to teach them
an important lesson. He is met by a "Canaanite woman." Now, this
label is important. At this stage of history, a person from this region
would no more be called a Canaanite than someone from Sweden
would be called a Viking. Jesus refers to her as Canaanite to show
the long enmity between the Israelites and Canaanites. As the
woman pleads for help, Jesus remains silent. His disciples know
that Jesus, a Jew, would not converse with a Canaanite or a woman.
He would have to cross two boundaries in order to speak to her. So,
they tell Jesus to send her away.

But Jesus speaks to her, crossing both boundaries. His words,
however, seem cruel: "I was sent only to the lost sheep of the house
of Israel." Jesus is not only dealing with this woman and her problem,
he is also teaching his disciples. Thus, he puts this woman to the
test. He is asking her, "Why should I, a Jew, help you, a Gentile?"
She kneels at Jesus' feet, with only one plea: "Lord, help me." Jesus'
response appears even more degrading: "It is not fair to take the

children's food and throw it to the dogs." This shocked the disciples. He is taking their own narrative ("God is for us, not them") to the extreme. As Kenneth Bailey notes, "It is acutely embarrassing to hear and see one's deepest prejudices verbalized and demonstrated."

Dogs, in Jesus' day, were almost as despised as pigs. They were not pets! Dogs wandered around like beggars looking for scraps. To neglect her request is one thing; to refer to her as a dog is another. How does she respond? "Yes, Lord, yet even the dogs eat the crumbs that fall from their masters' table." Brilliant! Jesus replies, "Woman, great is your faith! Let it be done for you as you wish." Her daughter was instantly healed. The disciples are watching carefully. Jesus has just given them a life-altering lesson. Again, Bailey notes, "An enormous amount of sophisticated spiritual formation is taking place in the hearts of the disciples and indeed potentially in the hearts of any readers of Matthew's Gospel."

Even when we think Jesus has veered from the truth, or is not doing something beautiful, or is not out for someone's good, rest assured. He is. Even if we do not see it at first.

When I think about the mystery of the incarnation, I am overwhelmed. I agree with Brian Zahnd: "Over time I have become obsessed with the sacred mystery of the Incarnation, and it is a magnificent obsession indeed. To think deeply about the Incarnation is sacred meditation." When I think deeply on the incarnation I am struck by the grace, mercy, and love of God. It's a sacred mystery that moves me to say both "wow" and "thanks." It's an amazing grace. The very act of the incarnation was in itself redemptive.

WHAT'S AT STAKE?

Seeing the incarnation in its fullness prevents us from reducing Jesus to either a mere teacher or a savior. Jesus came that we might have abundant life. He opened up the kingdom of God, restored

Israel, restored us, and taught us truth—the kind that can set us free if we continue in it. The story is much bigger and better, more profound and compelling, when we see the fullness of who Jesus is. By doing so, we see that the story is not a dry set of doctrines or laws, but an adventure. The magnificent story includes the amazing claim that God so loved us that he gave his only begotten Son, not merely to teach us or to forgive us but to shine through us.

Fyodor Dostoevsky once wrote, "If anyone could prove to me that Christ is outside the truth, and if the truth really did exclude Christ, I should prefer to stay with Christ and not with truth." The good news is that we don't have that problem. Jesus *is* the truth. And Jesus is beautiful and good. We can rely on him, we can live in awe of him, and we can be sure he will do good in our lives if we let him.

Soul Training Exercise
SMELL

THIS WEEK WE ARE CONTINUING to expand on our beauty journal by exploring the five senses and how God woos us with beauty through those senses. Each practice is meant to be creative and open, so you can make changes and do what you want, but I've offered suggestions if you are unsure what to do. With each practice, it is important to shift the focus from the beauty of what you are experiencing (the penultimate) to the Source of all beauty (the ultimate). This week we will focus on smell.

Smell exercise. Smell is a powerful sense deeply connected to memory. For this exercise, consider smells you associate with positive moments in your life. A friend associates the smell of smoke from extinguished candles with the peace and calm after her morning prayers. Another friend always wore patchouli, and whenever I smell it I remember him and smile.

As you go through your day, notice the good smells that surround you. The morning coffee brewing, the freshly mowed grass, the lotion your spouse wears, the candle wax, the roasted vegetables in the oven, the rain on the horizon. Allow each beautiful smell to be an invitation whispered to you from God, who loves you enough to create all these amazing things.

At the end of your day, or early the next morning, reflect on all those smells. Offer a prayer of gratitude to God for the beauty you experienced through your nose, and the love that is underneath those experiences.

Bonus practice. If you want to take a deeper look at Jesus and the gospel, read the Gospel of Mark. Mark is the shortest gospel, so you can read it in a single sitting. Pay attention to the *Christ-Form*, meaning, what you see in combination of the words and actions of Jesus. Also, pay attention to the words "amazed" or "astonished," which occur many times in Mark's Gospel. For fun, try to keep track of how many times they occur. Remember, we were made for a magnificent story, a story that should amaze and astonish us.

GOING THE DISTANCE

He has rescued us from the power of darkness and transferred
us into the kingdom of his beloved Son, in whom
we have redemption, the forgiveness of sins.

COLOSSIANS 1:13-14

WHEN MY WIFE, MEGHAN, came home from her sonogram, the look on her face frightened me. She couldn't speak for a few moments. Then she said, "The doctors think something is wrong with Madeline."

The doctors said the little girl inside of Meghan, whom we had named Madeline, might have a chromosomal disorder. They wanted to see us the next day for more tests. We spent that night in fear and trembling. After more tests, we waited alone in a room, praying. Two doctors came in the room and told us they suspected Madeline had a fatal chromosomal disorder.

"What does that mean?" Meghan asked.

"It means that your daughter will die, usually at birth," one of the doctors said with little emotion.

"Are you sure?" I asked.

"Based on our tests, it is most likely. We have an emergency C-section scheduled for tomorrow. You two need to make some decisions," the other doctor explained.

"What kind of decisions?" Meghan asked.

"Well, the most important one is whether you are willing to have a DNR," he said.

"What is a DNR?" I asked.

"It stands for 'Do Not Resuscitate.' There is a chance she will live—for a while. Once we know that she has trisomy 18 we know it is only a matter of time, so it is best not to use heroic measures to keep the child alive. It is more humane not to resuscitate," the doctor explained.

We sat in silence. We had recently finished painting her nursery. Now we were being asked whether or not to keep her alive. We had just built her crib. Now we were being forced to think about her coffin. There was nothing we could do. We felt utterly helpless. All we could do was wait for the next day—and pray. The only problem with the latter was that I felt hatred for God at that moment. How could God do this to us? We were faithful Christians.

After we went home, I told Meghan I need some time alone to pray. I really needed time alone to cry. I fell on the bed and began sobbing. The sobbing turned to crying, first for Maddie, for Meghan, and then for me. Then the anger surfaced. I began screaming at God.

"How could you do this to us! How could you make us decide whether to keep her alive? It's not fair!" I shrieked. "How *dare* you, God!" I seethed.

There was only silence. It was a piercing silence. The God who had spoken to me for the last seventeen years, whose presence I felt every day, had abandoned me in my darkest hour.

The next day we went to the hospital. The delivery went quickly, and Madeline came out alive, but not crying. The doctors whisked her away. I held Meghan's hand in silence. The doctors came back, and said they did not think she had trisomy 18, and that she would likely live.

"Live? How long?" we asked.

"Difficult to say," he said.

Madeline was later diagnosed with a rare chromosomal translocation, in which parts of two chromosomes had switched places. She would, they predicted, never thrive and grow, but she did exceed their prediction. She died one month after her second birthday. During her life she became our beloved Maddie, who we dearly loved. She also became my greatest teacher. Madeline made me look life's hardest questions in the face, not as theory but as reality. How could a good God do this? How could God make a world in which this could happen? Why does God allow evil and suffering?

Those questions are the subject of *theodicy*, which is the theological response to the problem of evil. Each day the innocent suffer. From Auschwitz to school shootings, we are faced with difficult questions: Did God cause this? Does God allow it? Could God have prevented it? Where was God? These are the hardest questions to answer for those who believe in a good and beautiful God. But there are answers. They are not found in theological textbooks but in the *grand and beautiful story*.

Have you experienced a traumatic event and wondered where God was in this event?

FALSE NARRATIVE

As Christians, we tend to focus on doctrines. Doctrines are soundbite statements of faith. The Trinity and the incarnation are important doctrines. They help us grasp mysteries. But as the great theologian Hans Frei maintained, doctrine is not the meaning of the story but rather the story is the meaning of the doctrine. Therefore, we should not build our faith on a series of doctrinal propositions, but on the whole story, and then let the doctrinal meaning come forth from it.

A great example of this mistake is the doctrine of penal substitution—the belief that Jesus' death on cross takes away the punishment we deserve because of our sin. The doctrine of penal substitution is not wrong. Our sins are real. We need forgiveness. Jesus really did erase "the record that stood against us with its legal demands. He set this aside, nailing it to the cross" (Colossians 2:14). The notion of penal substitution is amazing, as recorded in the wonderful hymn "It Is Well with My Soul."

> My sin, oh, the bliss of this glorious thought,
> My sin, not in part, but the whole,
> Is nailed to the cross and I bear it no more!
> Praise the Lord, praise the Lord, O my soul!

It is so glorious that it has eclipsed the rest of the story. And when it stands alone, it can end up telling the *wrong* story.

In his book *Simply Good News*, N. T. Wright uses an analogy to understand how this happened. Imagine that archaeologists discover a carved stone that is an ancient piece of art, a fragment of a larger picture. Perhaps it was from a temple. In this fragment a woman is looking off to her side at something in the distance. Not having the rest of the pieces, the archaeologists try to discover the story this piece of art is telling through analogous works they have seen. One of the archaeologists says, "Her face and her glance are similar to the ancient depictions of a processional to a sacrifice at the temple. She is glancing to her right, looking at the temple where animals will be sacrificed to appease the gods." This story makes sense to the group; they have seen it before.

Sometime later, however, the rest of the pieces of the carving are found. The archaeologists were wrong. The piece depicts a procession for the coronation of a new king. The woman in the picture is the new king's sister and is a part of the processional. She is glancing at her child, who has stopped to look at a bird. The archaeologists were right about it depicting a procession, but they were wrong about the kind of ceremony.

Wright believes this is similar to what happened to the way we understand the *fragment* of our larger story—the part of the story known as the *crucifixion*.

We take a beautiful, good, and true fragment (the crucifixion) and build the wrong story around it—Jesus was a sacrifice to appease an angry God. However, it is not *completely* wrong. The statement "Jesus died for our sins" is true. But the story built around the fragment is neither good nor beautiful, and thus distorts the whole truth of the statement "Jesus died for our sins." He did. But he was doing so much more.

Jesus died for our sins in the context of a different story. Therefore, his death must be interpreted another way. Just as in the archaeology analogy, the crucifixion was part of a procession, but not to a sacrifice as much as to a coronation. The death of Jesus was—to Paul and the early church—the crowning of a new King. Yes, he was the Lamb of God whose blood forgives sins, but that is only one aspect of the cross. He is not only the victim, he is the Victor, the new King, who now rules and reigns in his kingdom.

> *How do you respond to Wright's analogy? Is it a helpful explanation of how we can misunderstand the gospel?*

THE FULL EXTENT OF LOVE

Jesus knew his own death was imminent. He knew the weight of the world's sin was about to be laid on him. He anticipated the whipping, the scourging, and the beating. He knew he would enter the depths of alienation. The Creator and Sustainer of the universe was on his way to execution. He gave his full consent, without hesitation and with complete joy, because he knew he would take the place of the people, the object of his love. John 13:1 reads, "Having loved his own who were in the world, he now showed them the full extent of his love" (NIV 1984).

He would offer to the Father the divine yes in place of the human no. He would set them free, liberating them from the tyranny of shame and guilt, sin and death. Best of all, he knew he would bring them into fellowship with himself and the Father, through the Spirit. He was joyful because that is how lovers feel when they are about to rescue their beloved. The divine love story is about to reach its peak. Over the course of three days, he would show the full extent of his love, reconciling and rescuing his beloved.

The Trinity was on the move. The Trinity had a mission: to do for humankind what they could never do for themselves. This mission had begun in the incarnation. God was now walking the earth, feeling every human emotion and experience. The incarnation was the first saving act, the first act of the atonement. Salvation is more than getting into heaven after death. It's freedom from the enemies that destroy us: the law, which creates sin, which creates death. We face two other enemies: suffering and abandonment. In order to defeat them, God would have to die, and that would require "a body capable of death" (Athanasius). Everything was in place. Though they could not understand it, Jesus warned his friends this time would come. Jesus was about to reveal the depths of trinitarian love. This is the pinnacle of the great story.

THE KENOSIS OF HOLY WEEK

I have defined *kenosis* as the act of "self-sacrifice for the good of another." Creation was the first act of kenosis: God binds himself to us by creating us and this magnificent world. Covenant was the next act of kenosis: God binds himself to Israel in steadfast faithfulness, despite their infidelity. The incarnation was the next act of kenosis, in which God binds himself to humanity by becoming human.

The kenotic act by God that the world had seen happened in the incarnation. But now, the most extreme acts of kenosis are about to happen, on what we call Holy Week. The early church fathers called it *triduum mortis* (three-day death). On these three days Jesus will stand in solidarity with humankind, doing for us what we could never do. In trinitarian obedience, he will obey the Father, who calls him to experience the worst that humans are capable of (and that humans can experience). In so doing, the Trinity will rescue us from our enemies.

GOOD FRIDAY: THE FIRST ACT OF LOVE

And being found in human form, he humbled himself and became obedient to the point of death—even death on a cross. (Philippians 2:7-8)

The cross is the most recognized symbol in the world. The death of God is the most powerful moment in history. There are many ways to understand the work of atonement Jesus accomplished on the cross. There are many rich, theological words to describe it. The cross is God's act of *ransom* (buying a slave's freedom), *reconciliation* (a relationship is reestablished), *satisfaction* (required honor restored), an *appeal of love* (evoking a response of love from the beloved), and *substitution* (taking someone's place), to name a few.

The cross was such an amazing event that we need many ways to try to grasp its meaning.

Significantly, Jesus' death on the cross was a trinitarian act. In some versions of the gospel God the Father is angry and Jesus is trying to appease that wrath. Dallas Willard describes it this way:

> One of our main problems about the way the gospel is presented is it is often presented as if God were a pretty angry and mean Person, who is going to let you off the hook because someone else took your beating, namely Jesus. And we miss the point that it was the heart of love that sent Jesus. The death of Jesus on the cross did not make God happy, when he was unhappy. The death of Jesus on the cross was God's effort to reach human beings with his love. And because of what One member of that divine community did, God is enabled to reach out to human beings, and to say to them, "The war is over. You don't need to keep fighting." You don't need to carry on the battle any longer, because peace comes simply by accepting Jesus Christ and the God of Jesus Christ as real.

What a powerful statement!

Jesus' death forgives all sins "once for all" (Hebrews 10:10; 1 Peter 3:18). They are forgiven without a condition. Jesus' act on Good Friday proclaimed victory on our behalf. The finality of the cross was so comprehensive that Jesus would not have to repeat the act for future sins. Humanity, thanks to the cross, has been forgiven. It is up to each of us to choose to accept the gift.

What difference does it make if the arrangement is "Repent in order to be forgiven," and "You are forgiven, so repent"?

Jesus was on a rescue mission. He rescued us from evil, sin, and suffering. What more could Jesus have done for us? He has two more acts of love. One of them happened on Saturday—a day we often overlook.

HOLY SATURDAY: THE SECOND ACT OF LOVE

My friend Matt Johnson remarked that Holy Saturday has been almost completely overlooked in the church: "Saturday is not a day we commemorate what Jesus did for us, but has been turned into a day we spend preparing for Easter." What happened on Holy Saturday? According to the Bible and the early church, he "descended into hell." The Apostles' Creed is a summation of what Christians believe that first appeared in AD 390. It tells the magnificent story using short clauses, such as "he was conceived by the Holy Spirit, born of the virgin Mary." One overlooked clause is "he [Jesus] descended into hell." I have asked many Christians if they have heard this clause, and they admit to saying it. But when I ask if they know what it means, the response is nearly always, "No, I have never even thought about it." It is telling us something important about the story. In his descent, Jesus experienced extreme separation and alienation from God the Father. In his abandonment, he redeemed our times of abandonment. We need to understand it because it provides an answer to the problem of theodicy raised earlier.

Professor J. Warren Smith states it so well when addressing what the descent into hell on Saturday actually means. "It means there is no part of human existence to which Christ did not 'descend.'" And theologian Philip Clayton adds, "When I recite this in church, I think there is just no place where the encompassing love of God can't be present. There is no place where God is afraid to go."

It is a beautiful part of the magnificent story.

The *Anastasis* is an icon depicting Jesus' descent into Hades. It tells an extraordinary event. Jesus is at the center of the image. His robe is flowing upward to denote his rapid descent. He is standing on the golden doors of Hades, which he has just knocked down, denoting his conquering of death and hell. If you look closely you will see a chained skeletal figure: that is death or Satan. The enemy has been bound and killed by Christ. This depicts Hebrews 2:14: "that through death he might destroy the one who has the power of death, that is, the devil."

Perhaps my favorite part of the icon is Jesus pulling two people out of their graves: Adam and Eve. Though they were banished from the Garden for their transgression, Jesus now lifts them up from death as he eradicates their sin. Standing behind him are David and Solomon. They were Jesus' actual ancestors in the flesh.

Anastasis icon

I also love that right next to Jesus is John the Baptist, Jesus' forerunner in life and in death. There are Old Testament figures in the background, such as Elijah and Moses—who appeared at Jesus' transfiguration.

IS IT TRUE?

While this part of the story is good and beautiful, is it true? Several passages in the New Testament make reference to what the creed affirms. While the Gospels are largely silent about Holy Saturday, Jesus spoke about a time when "the dead will hear the voice of the Son of God, and those who hear will live" (John 5:25). Paul made mention of Jesus not only *ascending* but also *descending*: "'Who will descend into the abyss?' (that is, to bring Christ up from the dead)" (Romans 10:6-7), and "What does 'he ascended' mean except that he also descended to the lower, earthly regions?" (Ephesians 4:9 NIV). Finally, Paul wrote, "To this end Christ died and lived again, so that he might be Lord of both the dead and the living" (Romans 14:9).

Still, there is not much detail about what Jesus did on Holy Saturday. These verses from 1 Peter are more explicit:

He [Jesus] was put to death in the body but made alive by the Spirit, through whom also he went and preached to the spirits in prison who disobeyed long ago. (1 Peter 3:18-20 NIV 1984)

For this is the reason the gospel was preached even *to* those who are now dead, so that they might be judged according to men in regard to the body, but live according to God in regard to the spirit. (1 Peter 4:6 NIV 1984)

From these verses we learn that Jesus went to be with the dead, and that the gospel was preached to the dead.

The early church fathers affirmed the descent on Holy Saturday:

The Lord descended into the regions beneath the earth to preach his advent and to proclaim remission of sins for all who believe in him. (Irenaeus)

Christ went down into the deepest abysses of the sea, when he went into the Lowest Hell, to fetch forth the souls of his elect. (Gregory the Great)

The early church taught that Jesus descended to the place of the dead to preach good news and to set the captives free. My favorite explanation comes from one of the last of the church fathers, Isidore of Seville (seventh century). He writes, "Today he is, as king, come to the prison; today he has broken down the doors of bronze and has snapped the bolts of iron. He who, a dead man like any other, was swallowed up, has laid Hell to waste in God."

> *Have Jesus' actions on Holy Saturday been a part of your experience of God's redemption in your life? If they were, what impact would it make on you?*

Jesus went to lay hell to waste. This is affirmed by Jesus: "I am the Living One; I was dead, and now look, I am alive for ever and ever! And I hold the keys of death and Hades" (Revelation 1:18 NIV). On Holy Saturday, Jesus destroyed hell. He has taken on the wrath of God, he has defeated sin and death. Now Jesus takes one final step of kenosis in order to save us. He enters into a *second death*.

THE SPIRITUAL DEATH: ABSOLUTE SEPARATION

On Holy Saturday, Jesus willingly experienced complete and utter separation from the Father. This is referred to as the second death of Jesus. Jesus, who was cut off from human life on Friday, chooses to be cut off from God on Saturday. He has been obedient to the Father his entire life, but now he will engage in "the utmost pitch of obedience." Why? Hasn't he done enough?

Jesus died a complete death in order to experience complete abandonment by God. He does this so that he can experience—and thus redeem—the worst in human experience. He chooses to experience the utmost distance from God in order to overcome it. Just as he took on the guilt of sin and the wrath of God, now he takes on the absolute worst of human experience: abandonment. He first felt forsaken on Friday's cross; now he experiences complete forsakenness on Saturday's descent. Only trinitarian theology can help us begin to grapple with the idea of God being abandoned by God, but that is what Saturday is all about.

Holy Saturday was also the end of the reign of Satan. Hell was created as a kind of prison for Satan. On Friday, Satan rejoiced. He had gotten what he wanted: God's Son. Jesus descended to hell on Saturday to ruin the party. Just as in the Anastasis icon, Satan is bound and the dead are rescued. The great Reformer John Calvin wrote of Holy Saturday, "If it is left out, much of the benefit of Christ's death will be lost."

Elie Wiesel was a Romanian-born American Jewish writer, Nobel laureate, and Holocaust survivor. He told the story of the night he witnessed camp prisoners being hanged. The Nazi prison guards chose two men to be hanged, but also a child, just to show their power. Wiesel and others were asked to walk past the gallows and witness the scene. He describes what he saw:

> Then came the march past the victims. The two men were no longer alive. Their tongues were hanging out, swollen and bluish. But the third rope was still moving: the child, too light, was still breathing . . .

And so he remained for more than half an hour, lingering between life and death, writing before our eyes. And we were forced to look at him at close range. He was still alive when I passed him. His tongue was still red, his eyes not yet extinguished.

Behind me, I heard the same man asking: "For God's sake, where is God?"

And from within me, I heard a voice answer:

"Where He is? This is where—hanging here from this gallows . . ."

I am grateful that Jesus washed my sins away on the cross. But I am moved by our God who stands in solidarity with humans in the moments of the worst affliction we face—especially if it is forced on us by others.

SOLIDARITY IN OUR SUFFERING

When our daughter Madeline was diagnosed with a lethal disorder, we felt forsaken. We felt abandoned. On Holy Saturday Jesus entered into the kind of forsakenness and abandonment beyond anything any person could experience. He was not content to deal with our sin problem; his love extended into the worst of human suffering. Jesus felt what Meghan and I felt in our grief— and more. He not only redeemed human sin, he redeemed human suffering. And that is beautiful, good, and true. Summarizing Hans Urs von Balthasar's dialectic of the cross, Anne Murphy observes, "For the glory of God is most fully revealed in the descent of the Son into suffering, death and the passivity of the grave, that which is the *kenosis* of all beauty."

Jesus' actions on Holy Saturday offer us a way to understand how God can allow evil and suffering. God "accepted our foreknown abuse of freedom" in his "plan to take to himself our self-damnation in Hell." God is not a cosmic sadist who inflicts suffering on humans. He is a loving Savior who willingly enters into our suffering. I felt abandoned by God when we learned about our daughter's condition. Jesus felt and experienced a far worse abandonment. I felt alone and suffered in silence on many days. But Jesus, I now know, was with me all the time—in complete solidarity. He experienced it with and for me.

The apostle Paul was beaten and whipped, and was often imprisoned. From his jail cell he penned one of the most joyous pieces of literature ever written: his letter to the Philippians. In it he tells his reader about his one desire: "I want to know Christ and the power of his resurrection and the sharing of his sufferings by becoming like him in his death" (Philippians 3:10). I used to believe this meant we should seek suffering in order to be like Jesus. But Paul does not say he wants to share in his suffering; he wants to share in *Jesus'* suffering. I believe he wants to stand in solidarity with what Jesus suffered, just as Jesus stands in solidarity with our suffering.

One day I came upon a photo that helped me understand Holy Saturday. It showed the sacred heart of Jesus sketched on one of the walls inside of Auschwitz, perhaps the most horrifying of all of the Nazi concentration camps. With a large heart etched into the center of his chest, Jesus stands with extended hand and a look of compassion. I was overcome by the reality that someone scratched this into the wall in the midst of the worst suffering. Jesus now stands, as he did on Holy Saturday, in *that* place. Holy Saturday began in tragedy but would end in triumph, as Jesus defeated hell.

EASTER SUNDAY: THE THIRD ACT OF LOVE

After his death, Jesus' disciples went into hiding. They assumed it was over, and all of their hopes and dreams were destroyed. Then one morning three women went to his tomb to tend to his body. They were met by an angel: "'Don't be alarmed,' he said. 'You are looking for Jesus the Nazarene, who was crucified. He has risen!'" (Mark 16:6 NIV). Three powerful words that changed history: he has risen!

All that has been said so far—Jesus took away the guilt and shame of sin, drained the cup of wrath, defeated death, and vicariously transformed human suffering—would be meaningless were it not for the resurrection. Paul said it clearly: "If Christ has not been raised, our preaching is useless and so is your faith. . . . And if Christ has not been raised, your faith is futile; you are still in your sins. Then those also who have fallen asleep in Christ are lost" (1 Corinthians 15:14, 17-18 NIV).

Jesus' resurrection was a vindication of everything he had accomplished, particularly on these last three days. The issue is not the resurrection but *who* is resurrected. Lazarus was resurrected, only to die again. The fact that God died and was raised from the dead makes the resurrection not merely a grand miracle but a power great enough to transform the world.

> *What difference does it make to see the act of reconciliation and rescue not just as the work of Jesus but the unified work of the Trinity?*

The resurrection is the work of the Trinity. Jesus was utterly powerless in his death and ascent. The Father and the Spirit raised him: "Christ was raised from the dead by the glory of the Father" (Romans 6:4). The Trinity has completed its mission, so far, anyway. There is still more to the story.

A BEAUTIFUL, GOOD, AND TRUE RESCUE MISSION

Jesus did not reconcile God to us. Jesus reconciled us to God: "In Christ God was reconciling the world to himself, not counting their trespasses against them" (2 Corinthians 5:19). This distinction is important.

Jesus' mission was not to appease his Father by his death but to draw us to himself through the beauty, goodness, and truth of his death, descent, and resurrection (John 12:32). This is what Dostoevsky meant when he said, "Beauty will save the world." Jesus died in the cruelest of ways, under an empire of violence. He redeemed crucifixion by the power of his love. Brian Zahnd writes, "Every cross adorning a church is in itself a sermon—a sermon proclaiming that if Christ can transform the Roman instrument of execution into a thing of beauty, there is hope that in Christ all things can be made beautiful!"

Jesus descended to the dead to rescue those who were alienated from God. He experienced utter desolation and alienation from God in order to stand in solidarity with all who have experienced the same. He bore our sins on Friday, buried them in hell on Saturday, and defeated sin and death on Sunday. This isn't a courtroom drama, but a love story. Thomas Dubay describes this rescue mission well: "We have been created and redeemed for the eternal ecstasy of an interpersonal immersion in the triune God, seeing infinite Beauty face to face."

Seen in its wholeness the "three-day death" was much more than a rescue mission. It made a relationship with the Trinity possible. As Simon Chan says, "The Christian story is not primarily about how God in Jesus came to rescue sinners from some impending disaster. It is about God's work of initiating us into a fellowship and making us true conversational partners with the Father and the Son through the Spirit and, hence, with each other (1 Jn 1:1-4)." In Jesus' crucifixion, descent and abandonment, and resurrection, Jesus has made it possible for us to participate in trinitarian life.

As J. R. Briggs likes to say, "Because the tomb is empty, the pressure is off." We are now free from the law. We are forgiven forever. We suffer, but it now has meaning. The old has passed; the new has come. But we don't sit idly, enjoying God's work. As N. T. Wright says, "Jesus's resurrection is the beginning of God's new project not to snatch people away from earth to heaven but to colonize earth with the life of heaven. That, after all, is what the Lord's Prayer is about." We are invited to join the project. We are invited to participate in the story as it unfolds.

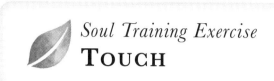

THIS WEEK WE ARE CONTINUING to expand on our beauty journal by exploring the five senses and how God woos us with beauty through those senses. Each practice is meant to be creative and open, so you can make changes and do what you want, but I've offered suggestions if you are unsure what to do. With each practice, it is important to shift the focus from the beauty of what you are experiencing (the penultimate) to the Source of all beauty (the ultimate). This week we will focus on touch.

Touch exercise. To experience the beauty of touch, find something soothing to touch. Perhaps you could sculpt something with Play-Doh, carve something in wood, work with the soil in your garden, or sew using a lush fabric.

Before you begin working with the material, take a few deep breaths and remember that God is present, and that God has proclaimed this material good!

As you work with the material, notice its weight, texture, resistance, and fluidity. Imagine Jesus sitting and observing the material with you. Consider the joy Jesus experienced as he, God in flesh, experienced these things himself growing up.

When you have finished, thank God for the touch of creation. Allow this penultimate beauty to draw you closer to the ultimate!

MAKING ALL
THINGS NEW

*If I find in myself a desire which no
experience in this world can satisfy, the most probable
explanation is that I was made for another world.*

C. S. LEWIS

ABOUT A YEAR AFTER I BECAME A CHRISTIAN, a friend invited me to his church to watch a Christian movie about the rapture. He said I should bring along friends who were not saved. The movie was *A Thief in the Night.* On the night the movie was showing, I saw a movie poster declaring *"And there will be no place to hide"* at the church entry. I felt a chill as I walked in and sat on a folding chair in the gym. In his greeting the pastor said the film was based on the Bible, particularly Matthew 24 and 1 Thessalonians 4. The movie, he said, depicted how the world would end. "Enjoy the show."

The movie is about Patty and her friends. An evil government has taken over the world and is forcing everyone to put a mark on their forehead. Without the mark a person can't use money and thus can't buy food or water. Ultimately, failure to take the mark could lead to execution. Patty, an occasional churchgoer, considers herself a Christian. But her family warns that she must accept Jesus or face the Great Tribulation. Patty can't make up her mind, and then one day she wakes up to find that her family, and millions of others, have disappeared in the rapture. She has been *left behind.*

The rest of the film is a terrorizing tale of evil and suffering during the Great Tribulation. People are executed by guillotine. In the movie, Larry Norman's song "I Wish We'd All Been Ready" is played. The film had a clear intent: to scare the hell out of people. Fortunately for me, I had accepted Jesus (in the right way, according to Fred). So I was safe. At the end the pastor offered salvation to anyone who would come forward. About twenty people did. I sat in my seat, with a deep sadness. *So, this is how it ends?* My understanding of the end times had been shaped by the film, and I would carry that narrative for many years.

Twenty-five years later the authors of the Left Behind book series said they were indebted to the film. The series title comes from the refrain in Norman's song. The film has been viewed by 300 million people worldwide. And the Left Behind series has sold over 65 million copies. In a Sunday school class I taught recently, this version of the end was by far the dominant narrative. One young woman had read the Left Behind series six times. The night I saw *A Thief in the Night,* the pastor said it was based on the Bible, so I assumed it was true. We will examine that later. For now I have two other questions. Is it a *beautiful* ending? Is it a *good* resolution to this magnificent story?

IS IT BEAUTIFUL AND GOOD?

In classic Christian liturgy there is a common affirmation called the Memorial Acclamation. It is recited by Lutherans and Catholics, Anglicans and Methodists, to name a few. The people make this bold assertion: "Christ has died, Christ is risen, *Christ will come again.*" The return of Jesus is a central tenet of the Christian faith. Everything about our story so far has been beautiful, good, and true. The return, the rapture, and the restoration of all things should also be beautiful, good, and true. When beauty is seen, it pleases. Is this a pleasant ending? I find this version of the return of Jesus, of how it all ends, unpleasant.

Instead of saying "wow" or "ahh," this Left Behind version of the end of all things makes me say "whoa" and "oh no." It is a story of violence. Whether you believe Christians will be taken before or after a time of tribulation, there is a tribulation. *Tribulation* is, by definition, a state of suffering, trial, trauma, and sorrow. This is hardly beautiful. If this film were anywhere close to what the end might be like, then there is nothing beautiful about it. In terms of genre, this would be considered a horror film. Dominance, control, and execution are not beautiful.

When experienced, goodness always benefits. Is the Left Behind version of the end good? Certainly not for those who get left behind. Perhaps it is good for those who are raptured, but the overall story is not one of benefit or benevolence. Judgment and punishment are delivered, and that in itself is not good. We must admit that there is great mystery in our story. The Trinity is a mystery. The incarnation is a mystery. The return of Jesus and the restoration of all things—including judgment—are also mysteries. I am certain, however, that the magnificent story will end as it began: beautiful, good, and true. When Dallas Willard was asked what the end will be like, he said, "Whatever God does in the end, we will think it's a great idea." I find comfort and encouragement in this.

IS IT TRUE?

The Left Behind version of how it all ends is neither beautiful nor good, so it must not be true. Unfortunately for the authors, singers, and movie makers, that story is not found in the Bible. It is connected to the shaming gospel. Therefore, I will refer to this as the "scary ending" story. Like the shaming story, it is built on misinterpretations of *two* passages: 1 Thessalonians 4:13-18 and Matthew 24:41.

> Then two will be in the field; one will be taken and one will be left. Two women will be grinding meal together; one will be taken and one will be left. (Matthew 24:40-41)

> The Lord himself, with a cry of command, with the archangel's call and with the sound of God's trumpet, will descend from heaven, and the dead in Christ will rise first. Then we who are alive, who are left, will be caught up in the clouds together with them to meet the Lord in the air; and so we will be with the Lord forever. Therefore encourage one another with these words. (1 Thessalonians 4:16-18)

The assumption of the scary ending is that these two passages are related. In Matthew, Jesus is assumed to be talking about the rapture, and then in Thessalonians Paul describes what will happen at the rapture. There are two problems with this. First, the word *rapture* is never found in the Bible. Second, each passage is taken out of context.

Let's start with the *rapture* theory. It is a relatively new doctrine. Amateur British theologian John Nelson Darby (1800–1882) began teaching *dispensationalism*—a theory of epochs in history—in the 1830s. In each epoch, he taught, God tests humanity or its representative, and they repeatedly fail and are judged. In the sixth epoch, things get worse and worse until Christ secretly returns and suddenly whisks away (raptures) all true believers to heaven, leaving the nonbelievers behind to suffer. The great preacher and evangelist D. L. Moody (1837–1899) agreed with Darby and used the rapture as a part of his revivalist preaching. In an 1887 sermon, Moody proclaimed, "I look on this world as a wrecked vessel. God has given me a life-boat, and said to me, 'Moody, save all you can.'" It would continue to take hold into the twentieth century and by the 1970s would be the standard teaching about the return of Jesus among many evangelicals and fundamentalists.

In addition to introducing a whole new doctrine (the rapture) with no biblical foundation, the second problem is that both passages are read out of context. The passage in Matthew is indeed about being ready for the end, but those who are taken away are not the righteous but the *unrighteous*, and they are being taken away to judgment. Jesus begins this section by discussing the wicked people in the time of Noah who were not ready to be swept away in the flood. This is a warning to the wicked, not a word of comfort to the believers. The believers *stay* on the earth. Darby had the wrong people flying to heaven.

In 1 Thessalonians the issue Paul is addressing is whether those who have died prior to the return of Jesus are at a disadvantage. Paul wants to "encourage" (v. 18) the Thessalonian Christians with this passage. His pastoral point is that the dead are not at a disadvantage. Paul's term for the return of Jesus is called the *parousia*. *Parousia* was used to describe an imperial visit by a king to a city. People would send a delegation outside the city gates to greet the dignitary. Those who went out to meet the dignitary always *returned* with the dignitary into their city. So Paul is describing "an escort to earth." When Jesus returns, those who are alive will rise to greet him and accompany him on his descent. Then the dead in Christ will rise to meet them. In other words, it is a big party—on earth.

THE BEST KEPT SECRET IN THE BIBLE

If you ask most Christians what will happen after they die, they would likely say, "We will live in heaven forever." If you followed up with "And where is heaven?" they would likely say, "Way, way far away." That is the general assumption.

So, let me state this clearly and boldly: *not one* New Testament passage claims that Christians will live forever in heaven. I realize that this will leave many readers shocked, because that narrative is deeply embedded in the minds of most people. In cartoons, movies, jokes ("So a guy dies and goes to heaven and meets St. Peter at the Pearly Gates . . ."), and television ads, heaven is depicted as a fluffy place. Usually there are clouds and harps, and no one seems to have anything to do except float around the fluffy place. Again, this is not found in the Bible. Neither expectation—a faraway heaven, a place to float around—is supported by Scripture nor taught in the early church. The good news is that what the Bible *does* teach is much better.

The Bible's teaching about the end is this: God, in Jesus, will create *new heavens and a new earth*. This is the Bible's best kept secret, even though the Bible is consistent, clear, and unambiguous about this. It is even found in the Old Testament. Isaiah speaks of this in several places:

> For as the new heavens and the new earth,
>   which I will make,
> shall remain before me, says the LORD;
>   so shall your descendants and your name remain.
>   (Isaiah 66:22)

The people of Israel, as well as the early Christ-followers, expected a complete restoration, a transformation so complete that we can only guess at how marvelous it will be.

Jesus affirms the new heavens and new earth understanding in several places, notably referring to it as "the renewal of all things" in Matthew 19:28. All things will be renewed when Jesus is finally seated on his throne. His apostles proclaimed the same, proclaiming it as the "universal restoration" (Acts 3:20-21). In this passage Peter connects the universal restoration to Old Testament prophecy. He believed the new heavens and the new earth were promised by God (2 Peter 3:13). In Hebrews we learn that God is going to prepare a city for his people. The idea of the *city* as a part of the new heavens and the new earth is explained in the book of Revelation.

WHAT REVELATION REALLY TEACHES

The book of Revelation, or the Apocalypse of John, is where most Christians turn to discover how it all ends. But Revelation is a difficult book to understand because it was written for both the second century and the future. Much of the book describes the coming tribulations Christians will face under Roman persecution. Those passages are not referring to things that will happen in a thousand years or more. Speculation about "the beast" or its mark is futile for us today because *they already happened*. Nearly all of the symbols and characters mentioned dealt with first-century events. Books written by New Testament scholars confirm this. (I recommend Paul Spilsbury's *The Throne, the Lamb & the Dragon* and Craig Koester's *Revelation and the End of All Things*.)

The book of Revelation does speak about the *future* and what it will be like, but not in the first twenty chapters. The references to the future are in Revelation 21–22, which are explicit in their affirmation of the great renewal: "Then I saw a new heaven and a new earth; for the first heaven and the first earth had passed away, and the sea was no more" (Revelation 21:1). From Genesis to Revelation the Bible is clear about the end: God will make all things new—that is, just the way they were intended to be.

The renewal of all things began at the resurrection. It will find its completion in a new heaven and a new earth. N. T. Wright explains,

> God is not going to abolish the universe of space, time and matter; he is going to renew it, to restore it, to fill it with new joy and purpose and delight, to take from it all that has corrupted it. . . . New creation has begun in Jesus. There is a pilgrim highway leading all the way from the cross and the empty tomb right through to God's new creation.

The earth will be renewed, and the heavens will be cleansed. How will the heavens be renewed? At present there are dark spiritual forces, but they will be fully defeated at Christ's return. Isn't that good and beautiful? According to the Bible, it is also true.

There is continuity between our present heavens and earth and the new heavens and new earth. What will it be like? We have only one thing on which to base our answer: Jesus' resurrected body. When Jesus appeared to Mary and his disciples after he rose, he appeared to them in a body. It was a physical body (they could touch his wounds, and he ate breakfast with them on the beach), but it was altogether new. He was not immediately recognizable to them. He could also walk through a wall. His physical body had been radically transformed. That is true of the new earth. It's the same earth, but radically transformed. It will be good, beautiful, and true.

Simon Chan observes, "The church is part of an unfolding story whose end has already been anticipated in the resurrection and whose historical finale will be . . . a 'eucatastrophe.'" A catastrophe is sudden event that causes damage and harm. But a *eucatastrophe* is "a sudden and *favorable* resolution of events in a story." Our magnificent story will have a favorable ending. From the opening act of creation to the resurrection and ascension, God has been telling a story that is so beautiful and good and true that the end could be none other than beautiful, good, and true. We will say of this ending, "What a great idea."

THE RESCUED RESCUE

The rapture and the fluffy heaven story have no interest in *this world*. The scary ending story is merely a great escape from this world. The fluffy heaven story is one of individualism and isolation. The only thing that matters is *not* to be left behind in this cosmic dump. How different was Jesus' message about the kingdom of God? In the kingdom of God—the with-God life together—we are on a mission to rescue, restore, and heal the world. Jesus' parable of the good Samaritan is a great metaphor for how we view this world. The priest and the Levite both passed by the injured man. But the Samaritan saw the beaten and robbed man, and felt pity. He took care of the man at his own expense.

Those who are awaiting a rapture, or have punched their heaven ticket and are awaiting death to get there, are like the priest and the Levite who look at this world—and the people in it—as something unclean and not to be troubled by because they are concerned only with leaving it. But as N. T. Wright notes, "The living God has come with healing and hope in Jesus Christ, has picked up the battered and dying world, and has bound up its wounds and set it on the road to full health." The great story is about a loving God who dares to offer humans "the responsible exercise of power on God's behalf over our earthly environment." Keas Keasler says,

"The great hope of Christianity is not that we get to escape all the suffering of the world, *but that God is going to use us to be a part of his healing project.* . . . If we shrink the gospel and make it just a message about individuals going to heaven, then the church can't help but become a sanctuary and hiding place from the world."

Those who have died and risen with Jesus are resurrection people, and as such are now partners in redeeming this world, not abandoning it. Christ-followers are called to be engaged with the renewal of human culture—on earth, as it is in heaven. As J. Richard Middleton points out, "To focus our expectation in an otherworldly salvation has the potential to dissipate our resistance to societal evil and the dedication needed to work for the redemptive transformation of this world." The resurrection is the sign of hope that all will end well. But in the meantime, those of us who dwell in the kingdom of God are inspired by divine energies to pray and serve and love and rescue and restore this world. This is the work we do in this life.

THE SENSE OF AN ENDING

Life is short, and we can accomplish only so much. Much of what we do will remain unfinished. For now. In one of my favorite short stories of all time, "Leaf by Niggle," author J. R. R. Tolkien provides us with a fascinating idea of what we might be doing in the next life. And it is not floating on clouds playing harp music! It is an unforgettable story about Niggle, a man whose passion is painting trees. The only problem is that Niggle is too distracted to paint the whole tree; he spends all his time painting leaves. He is never satisfied with the leaves he has painted, so he works on them endlessly. He never gets past the leaves! One day Niggle dies and awakens in an unfamiliar place. He comes upon a bicycle with a yellow label tied to the bars with "NIGGLE" written on it.

Niggle gets on the bicycle and begins riding through the meadow. He looks ahead and sees something so startling he falls off the bicycle. He sees *the* tree, the tree he had been painting his whole life but never finished. Here it is, finished! And it was not a painting; it was alive, real, swaying in the wind. Niggle had so often wondered how it would look. He gazes at the tree in wonder, slowly lifts his arms in praise, and utters, "It is a gift." What did Niggle realize? That his art—the work he did in his life—was a gift. But even more, he discovers that the work he did in his life would find its full completion in the life to come. St. Paul said as much in his letter to the Corinthians: "Therefore, my beloved, be steadfast, immovable, always excelling in the work of the Lord, because you know that in the Lord your labor is not in vain" (1 Corinthians 15:58).

As Balthasar put it so beautifully,

> In the "new heaven and the new earth" nothing that has ever been done or suffered in true self-abandonment will be lost. . . . All the treasures of the world will be brought into it. But they will be more beautiful and more precious than they were here because God's grace will perfect in them what we would have wanted to express but were not able to.

That is what Niggle got to experience: God's grace perfected his work on earth. That is why all Niggle could say was, "It is a gift."

I once asked Dallas Willard if I would ever understand the meaning of Madeline's condition and short life. Dallas said, "Perhaps in this life you will get a glimpse, but in the next life it will all make sense."

It is not only true of our work but also of our relationships.

We, especially Meghan, poured so much into this one little life that was cut short. I would like to think that Madeline will greet us when we come to the final restoration, and we will see, like Niggle, her life completed as it would have been. Like Niggle, I expect to stand in wonder before her, and she will look as I have guessed or imagined, but could never see. When that happens, I will gaze at her, slowly lift my arms open wide, and say over and over, "It's a gift." Wouldn't that be beautiful and good?

The apostle John wrote, "There will be no more night; they need no light of lamp or sun, for the Lord God will be their light, and they will reign forever and ever" (Revelation 22:5). We will *reign*. That is *dominion* language, the language we encountered in Genesis 1:26-28. We were designed for dominion. We were created to live well, to design, to create, to govern, and to build. The things we love in this life we will love in the next. For me that will include music, literature, poetry, food, friendship, writing, play, and laughter. I believe the work we engage in during this life will find its fulfillment in the next. For now, we can learn to see this life, this earth, and things we see and smell and taste and touch as sacraments pointing to something greater.

THE SACRAMENT OF THE PRESENT MOMENT

In this life we see a lot of pain and suffering. But we also see moments of beauty, goodness, and truth. We see people loving one another, sacrificing for one another, serving one another, and blessing one another. There is more beauty, goodness, and truth around us than we can perceive. I think this life is a journey in which we heal our eyes, as Augustine said, so that we can see the wonder of it all. I love witnessing reconciliation between enemies, forgiveness extended by those who have been harmed, and peace established where there once was strife. I love my family and my friends. I love my dog, Winston. He greets me every morning and evening with a wagging tail of enthusiasm.

My family is very close with another family, the Reads. We are more than friends; we are more like family. Cindy Read, the matriarch, calls us "framily." Gary and Cindy Read have three grown children. We all get together on a regular basis. We share great meals (Gary and his barbecue are a thing of beauty), play games, swim, sometimes dance, and always laugh. One gorgeous summer afternoon, while playing a lawn game, Nathan Read turned to me and asked, "So, Doc, what do you think the next life will be like?"

"Well, Nate," I said, "the Bible doesn't say a lot about what it will be like, and when it does, it uses imagery, like streets of gold, walls studded with gems. So it is hard to know. What do you think it will be like?" I asked.

Nathan surveyed the big backyard, with his family and friends enjoying life and one another. He looked at me with a big grin and said, "*This.*" To be clear, these moments are not identical instances of the next life. They must be seen, as all beautiful things must be seen, as *penultimate*, not *ultimate*. We are to experience them with gladness, and then turn in gratitude to the One who made them. Scot McKnight refers to these moments as *sacraments*: "Life's pleasures—success at work, a good meal, a beautiful song, satisfying sex, a splendid aroma—are sacraments, yes sacraments, of the new Heavens and earth." The present moments of life are sacraments if we have the eyes to see and the heart to feel them.

We have been exploring the gospel as a *story*, not as a set of doctrines or propositions or laws or theories. We are all made for a great story, but instead we often have been offered a shrunken gospel story. The great story that somehow has been forgotten is a story that stands up to the demands of the transcendentals of beauty, goodness, and truth. From creation to the return, the Trinity—the hero of our story—has told a story like no other. Every part of the story got better than the one before.

This notion of the story getting better as it goes on reminds us of the very last lines of the last book in the Chronicles of Narnia. In these final sentences, Aslan explains to the Pevensie children what it all has meant:

> He no longer looked to them like a lion; but the things that began to happen after that were so great and beautiful that I cannot write them. And for us this is the end of all the stories, and we can most truly say that they all lived happily ever after. But for them it was only the beginning of the real story. All their life in this world and all their adventures in Narnia had only been the cover and the title page: now at last they were beginning Chapter One of the Great Story which no one on earth has read: which goes on forever: in which every chapter is better than the one before.

Every chapter is better than the one before. That is what the never-ending magnificent story is all about. Even if in this life we have suffered greatly, we know it only gets better—because the tomb is empty. Our story is one of hope. It rests on the certainty proclaimed long ago by Julian of Norwich: "All shall be well, and all shall be well, and all manner of things shall be well."

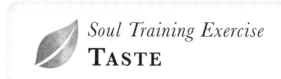

Soul Training Exercise
TASTE

THIS WEEK WE ARE CONTINUING to expand on our beauty journal by exploring the five senses and how God woos us with beauty through those senses. Each practice is meant to be creative and open, so you can make changes and do what you want, but I've offered suggestions if you are unsure what to do. With each practice, it is important to shift the focus from the beauty of what you are experiencing (the penultimate) to the Source of all beauty (the ultimate). This week we will focus on taste.

Taste exercise. To experience beauty, we often must slow down and become present to the moment. In our fast-food society, the beauty of tasting may be the most difficult to retrieve. For this exercise, set aside time to prepare and enjoy a meal you know you will enjoy. For extra credit, prepare and share the meal with someone you care about!

Bless the meal with gratitude to God for the provision of this meal and the wonder of taste and smell working together to gladden the heart. Then throughout the meal, practice noticing your food. Eat slowly, savoring each bite before you scoop up the next portion. If possible, add courses to your meal with space between to savor what you just enjoyed. And take time to name with others at the table what you notice about the food that makes it delicious. This could include the contrast of sweet and savory, mild and hot, as well as texture. Where and how do you notice these tastes in your mouth?

At the conclusion of the meal, offer a prayer of gratitude to God, naming all the wonders of this meal. Be specific and allow yourself to joyfully celebrate this expression of God's care for you.

Bonus exercise. Before you have your meal, watch the movie *Babette's Feast*. If you have been going through *The Magnificent Story* with a group, it would be great to watch the film together and then plan on having your own feast. The movie has a powerful point about enjoying life, especially a great meal, in contrast to the mistaken (often Christian) notion that God prefers that we live bland (and often sad) lives.

LIVING IN THE MAGNIFICENT WAY

He had been instructed in the Way of the Lord;
and he spoke with burning enthusiasm and taught
accurately the things concerning Jesus.

ACTS 18:25

W E GOT OUR DOG, WINSTON, from a breeder when he was seven weeks old. The breeder asked us to bring an old towel with us when we first met him. She told us to rub the towel on our skin. We didn't know why, but we did it. We played with him for half an hour, and then the breeder said, "He is only seven weeks old, and he has never slept in a kennel alone. He can come home with you when he can go through the night in his kennel without crying. I will put the towel over his kennel at night so he can get used to your smell. It will comfort him and will ease the transition when he comes to live with you."

We were elated when, only two days later, the breeder called and said he had slept through the night without even a whimper. We rushed to her house and brought Winston home. He slept in his kennel that night and never cried. He went on to sleep in his kennel every night and still does to this day. He loves his kennel. At night, when he is tired, he goes to the kennel on his own. When we leave the house we simply say, "Winston, kennel up," and he goes right to it. He feels safe, and he trusts that we will let him out, feed him, pet him, and play with him.

We made a decision to raise him properly, with consistent training (and no people food!). Winston was not going to be a dog who merely lived in our house. He was going to be our companion. I was committed to taking an active role in his life. I regularly take Winston to the dog park, which he loves. As soon as I say "dog park," he runs to the front door, wagging with excitement.

When we go to the dog park, I like to walk or jog around the perimeter, which is about a half mile, so it is a pretty big space. Sometimes there are as many as twenty other dogs running around and playing with each other. When I walk around the park, Winston keeps an eye on me. He will play with another dog for a while, but when he sees I have gotten more than fifty yards away, he runs to catch up with me. He runs along with me for a while, and then, seeing another dog, he runs with it for a while. Then he will catch up with me once again. This happens over and over.

Winston is demonstrating a skill called *object constancy*. It is usually used to describe children who are well cared for. It is the ability to feel safe even when one's caregiver is not immediately in sight. Most children develop it when they are two or three years old. Assuming that key people in their world are reliable, over time children develop a sense that when Mom or Dad leaves the room, they have not vanished but will reappear again.

Winston feels safe with me. He knows I love him, I will his good, and I care for and protect him. When he gets ear infections, I get him medicine, pin him down (he is not a fan of being pinned), apply the medicine, rub it in for thirty seconds, and it is cured. Occasionally we run into a dog at the park who growls at, and sometimes even attacks, Winston. As soon as it happens he looks for me. Every time we go to the dog park, I think about what it means to enter the magnificent story: *I want to be like Winston. I want to love to be with God. I want to trust God like Winston trusts me. I want to long to be with God like Winston longs to be with me. I want his loyalty, his freedom, and his playfulness. I want his presumption.*

THE MAGNIFICENT WAY

The early Christians did not refer to their religion as "Christianity." In fact, they didn't refer to themselves as "Christians." They thought of themselves as "disciples." The word *disciple* appears 269 times in the New Testament; the word *Christian* appears only three times— and each time it is used to describe a disciple. I think Dallas Willard's definition is the best: "a disciple is an *apprentice* of Jesus in Kingdom living." The early Christ-followers didn't think they were a part of a religion. Instead, they referred to themselves as people on the *Way* (Acts 18:25; 19:9, 23).

That word makes sense. They stepped into a magnificent story, and it set them on a magnificent way, a magnificent journey. I like the word *journey* because it denotes an adventure. The aim of this book has been to tell the magnificent story in a new way, through beauty, goodness, and truth. As mentioned, we are all longing for a great story. The shrunken, fear-based, works-based stories have had their day. They have proven too weak to transform the human heart and, in turn, transform the world.

I look at our churches and see sad, frustrated, lonely people. Or I see churches whose aim seems to be maintaining their own success, not the magnificent way of Jesus. I see far too little real discipleship, and far too much self-centeredness. I see far too much pride and far too little power. We long to orient ourselves by a narrative larger than ourselves, just as we innately long for beauty, goodness, and truth. I think this has occurred because we have not heard the magnificent story.

THE MAGNIFICENT INVITATION: LIVING AS APPRENTICES OF JESUS

During our home remodeling we hired countless subcontractors, from electricians to plumbers to masons to framers. On several occasions I noticed that the subcontractors had apprentices. The subcontractors are seasoned professionals who have learned how to do their job well over time. The apprentices are new to the job and are learning the trade, not just through textbooks but by experience. One of the subcontractors, Wes, who is a framer, is having his sons learn the trade. He has them watch what he does, and he explains what he is doing at the same time. Then he lets them do the task themselves. It is a beautiful thing to watch. In the old days, when an apprentice finally mastered the job, the smiths (blacksmiths, ironsmiths, silversmiths) would say, "The trade has *entered* him."

This is exactly what Jesus is offering us. He is the master Teacher, and we are his apprentices. The magnificent story naturally leads us to be Jesus' apprentices. Unlike the other shrunken stories, the magnificent story is designed for us to enter into it, and thus to have the story *enter* us. This is a beautiful thing to see.

My friends Matt and Catherine Johnson have been living in the magnificent story for many years now. They exhibit Christlikeness in all they do. Their lives are oriented to the story through their practices. They are committed to their own lives with God, but they are also committed to their community. They intentionally live in a lower-income part of the city and are building relationships within their neighborhood. The magnificent story has entered them, and they are now its witnesses. They are on the magnificent way.

WE KNOW STUFF

In the past fifty years the church has ceded knowledge to the academy or the university. We have now been relegated to people who have *faith* but not real knowledge. The academy and the sciences are thought to be the only dispensers of real knowledge. This simply is not true. We in the church possess significant knowledge. For one thing, we have the magnificent story. We know about the Trinity. We know that creation is more than mere matter; it is beautiful and is a sign of the Storyteller's love. We know that there is an innate longing for goodness in human beings, and we know where it comes from. We know that Jesus spoke—and is—the truth. We know that God so loved the world that he gave his Son to rescue it. We know that Christ has died, Christ is risen, and Christ will come again.

I tell pastors, "If you have a church sign, put this on it: We Know Stuff." Because we really do know stuff. We know the kinds of things people are longing to know. Yes, we *believe* in God the Father almighty, maker of heaven and earth, but we believe it because we *know* it. Knowledge always precedes faith. When we know something, we can act on it. Knowledge is the ability to re-present something in an appropriate manner. I know the game of tennis. I am actually a certified instructor. I have played it for years. Even after not playing for a year, I can grab a racquet and play the game decently. Tennis has *entered* me. I know it in my head. (I can explain how to keep score and how to hold a Western grip.) But I mostly know it in my body. Most knowledge is experiential and bodily.

Belief is acting on what we know. Jesus is as real to me as the chair I am sitting on. Remember, reality is what we always bump into when we are wrong. I have heard the magnificent story and have been studying it, reflecting on it, contemplating it, marveling over it, and living it for some time. It works. It is real. It is true, and good, and beautiful. It is captivating. And as I come to know it, I trust it. Like my dog, Winston, I am learning *object constancy*. Now, when I face dark valleys, I am not nearly as afraid, because I know the good Shepherd is with me. He has been with me in the light, and I trust he is with me in the darkness.

Like Winston, I am learning to be *presumptuous*. I assume God loves me, cares for me, and protects me. I am living with God in the strong and unshakeable kingdom. I know stuff. And I believe stuff. Faith is an extension of knowledge; it is based on knowledge. We do not take leaps *of* faith, we take leaps *with* faith. Peter said, "May grace and peace be yours in abundance in the knowledge of God and of Jesus our Lord" (2 Peter 1:2).

Grace is God's action in our lives. It is more than mere forgiveness of sins, though it includes that as well. Grace is what we experience when we take a step in faith. When I open the Bible and invite the Spirit to speak to me, I am doing so in faith. And that faith is based on knowledge. I have come to know about the Bible and how the Spirit works.

Peace also comes from knowing the story. Peace, or *shalom*, is not merely the absence of conflict but the presence of the Trinity, who leads to harmony, wholeness, completeness, prosperity, welfare, and tranquility. That is why Peter can offer his blessing: as we come to know and live into the story, we experience grace and peace in abundance. Because we are coming to know God and Jesus our Lord—not in a book but in real life, in real time. The more we know, the more we grow in the fruit and power of the Spirit.

THE MAGNIFICENT JOURNEY IS A REVOLUTION

Cornelius Plantinga refers to the fall as the "vandalism of shalom." We know there is sin and brokenness in our world and in our hearts. But we also know that Jesus started a revolution. He is the greatest revolutionary who has ever lived. Dallas Willard described it this way: "The aim of God in history is the creation of an all-inclusive community of loving persons, with himself included in that community as its prime sustainer and most glorious inhabitant." Dallas's prayer, one that he said so often, was "I pray that you would have a rich life of joy and power, abundant in supernatural results, with a constant clear vision of never-ending life in God's world before you, and the everlasting significance of your work day by day, and that you would live a radiant life and a radiant death."

This is a coherent vision of the world, a goal to die for, a call to fraternity, and a call to mission. When we hear and enter the magnificent story, we are embarking on a magnificent journey. On this journey we become people who know, people of faith, people of hope, people of joy, people of peace, people of wisdom, and people of power. Jesus said a good tree will bear good fruit. Living into the story makes us good trees, and thus we will, without effort, bear good fruit. And finally, we will embark on a magnificent mission. As apprentices of the most revolutionary revolutionist, Jesus, we will be called and sent by the master Storyteller to bring the good news to the captives, the blind, and the imprisoned.

It will be *magnificent*.

ACKNOWLEDGMENTS

Though I never met him, I want to give thanks to Hans Urs von Balthasar. Balthasar was a twentieth-century Catholic theologian living in Switzerland. He wrote a sixteen-volume opus on understanding God and the gospel through the lenses of beauty, goodness, and truth. I began reading Balthasar in 2011. Only Dallas Willard compares as one whose thoughts shaped my own, opening me up to a new way of understanding our faith and moving me to doxology on nearly every page.

I would like to thank many people for helping make this book a reality. First, my editor, Cindy Bunch, and my agent, Kathy Helmers. They heard me speak on this topic years ago and asked over dinner, "Can you write a book on this subject? I think people would benefit from it." Their initial and continuing belief carried me through this project. It simply would never have made it to print without these two fine women.

Thank you to the many readers of early chapters who helped me understand what I was trying to say and how to say it as best I could. First, the initial group who met for many engaging Sunday mornings at Chapel Hill UMC in Wichita: Arlene Amiss, Aeramie and Tyler Porter, Bob and Arlo Casper, Dan Bennett and Jenny

Bennett, Dena Roney, Laura Peck, Josh and Jill Luton, Craig and Laurie Rhodes, Matt Brane, Hope Smith, Zach Morris, Matt and Catherine Johnson. Second, thank you to my final reading group, who helped shaped the final version of this book: Bob and Malaura Epperson, Trevor and Jen Hinz, Meghan Smith, Mark and Marita Soucie, Keas and Sarah Keasler.

I also want to thank Jim and Jenny Knight, who graciously allowed me to stay at their cabin in Ord, Nebraska, where I was able to write for eight days in order to finish the second draft of this book.

Special thanks also to my colleagues Dr. Stan Harstine (Bible scholar) and Dr. Chris Kettler (theologian). These two fine men took the time to read this book, helping to ensure that I avoid biblical or theological missteps. In addition, thanks to Ben Davis, who made helpful suggestions to me when we bumped into each other at Eighth Day Books. And it goes without saying, thanks to the bookstore owner Warren Farha, who, as he has done for every book I have written, provided me with suggestions for helpful books to read.

Finally, to my family—Meghan, Jacob, and Hope—who endured my long absences and supported me along the way. Especially Meghan, who was a champion of this book, honest critic, and never-ending cheerleader along the way.

STUDY GUIDE

by Matt Johnson

CHAPTER 1: LONGING FOR A MAGNIFICENT STORY

Gathering

As chapter one begins, the author writes, "We were made not just to enjoy stories but to enter them. We long to take our lives, our stories, and merge them with another story." As a group, share your favorite stories. And if you are willing, discuss where you find yourself in that story (perhaps you relate to one of the characters, the storyline, or the setting).

Exploring

1. The author asks, "What story have you been told about God? What have you been told about the gospel or about the Christian life, about Jesus, about the cross, about who you are, or about heaven?" Take a few minutes to consider how you would answer this question, or maybe one part of it (for example, about the Christian life). If you are comfortable, share your answer with the group.

2. The author gives definitions for the three transcendental virtues of beauty, goodness, and truth.

   • Beauty is that which, when seen, pleases.

- Goodness is that which works for the benefit or betterment of another.

- Truth is that which, when encountered, works.

1. As you consider these three definitions, how are they helpful to your understanding of these virtues?

2. What questions do you still have about beauty, goodness, and truth? These questions may not be answered immediately, but naming them as you move forward with the book may be helpful.

3. Reflect on a time beauty "stopped you in your tracks." If you are comfortable, share this with others.

4. The author explores the topic of relativism and postmodernity in relation to beauty, goodness, and truth. What has been your experience, good or bad, with relativism? How does the author's approach to this topic help you? What questions still remain?

5. In telling the story of Vedran Smailović, the cellist of Sarajevo, the author writes, "In the midst of tragedy, his music echoed from another world, a place where beauty, goodness, and truth reside. Through Smailović, an instrument of God, I believe, the people found hope and healing." When have you experienced beauty, goodness, and truth in the midst of suffering and pain? How did it affect you?

Engaging

The author utilizes 1 Corinthians 13:4-8 to discuss the nature of goodness and how it relates to beauty and truth. Take a few minutes to reflect silently on this passage, reading it through a few times.

Love is patient; love is kind; love is not envious or boastful or arrogant or rude. It does not insist on its own way; it is not irritable or resentful; it does not rejoice in wrongdoing, but rejoices in the truth. It bears all things, believes all things, hopes all things, endures all things.

Love never ends.

1. What words would you highlight in this passage as descriptions of goodness?

2. How can this Scripture help us to see beauty?

3. When have you seen this Scripture proven to be true?

Reflecting

The soul training exercise is designed to make you aware of the beauty that surrounds you. These questions will help you explore this exercise.

1. If you are comfortable, share with your group how you engaged with this exercise. Did you write in a journal, use a photo journal, or do something else? When did you do the exercise (morning, evening, randomly)?

2. What were the most powerful experiences of beauty you noticed throughout your week?

3. Were you able to move from the penultimate (the thing of beauty) to the ultimate (God)? Explain. How did you express your gratitude to God?

Closing

End your time together by reading this quote aloud:

Profound stories remind us that beauty, goodness, and truth are intertwined. I believe when we grasp this, we get a new and amazing understanding of what life with God can really be like. Hearing the good news of the gospel is similar to crying over the beauty of heavenly music. Experiencing the good news of the gospel is similar to feeling glad when we see someone perform an unexpected act of kindness for a stranger. The greatest news of all is that this is what *God* is like.

CHAPTER 2: FALLING FOR SHRUNKEN STORIES

Gathering

The author opens chapter two by discussing his own exposure to two shrunken gospels, the "do good works" gospel and the "shaming and scary" gospel. Without judgment or condemnation, spend time sharing with each other which of these gospels formed your background. What have been the drawbacks and limitations of the gospel you grew up with? What has been helpful about the gospel you grew up with (even if it was limited)?

Exploring

1. In the author's opening story of attending the church meeting, his pastor ended the meeting by saying, "Life is an endless search, and you never reach any kind of certainty." How might this belief affect a person's faith journey?

2. What is your reaction to the conversation the author had with Fred, who worked with a parachurch ministry for college students? Have you had similar conversations? If so, what were they like?

3. The shriveled story of the shaming gospel is this: "You are bad, God is mad, but Jesus took your beating. So try harder and you might make it to heaven." When have you been exposed to this gospel? How has it shaped you?

4. The author works through the four primary Scriptures of the

Roman Road. Discuss as a group if you have seen the four points of this tract before. What is your reaction to the presentation of the tract's Scriptures in their fuller context?

5. At the conclusion of the chapter, the author explains how the social gospel and the shaming gospel have several things in common, which are also their weaknesses. As you look at the list on page 31, which point is most surprising to you? And which point is least meaningful to you? Why?

Engaging

Read aloud the story of the call of the first disciples from Luke 5:1-11.

Once while Jesus was standing beside the lake of Gennesaret, and the crowd was pressing in on him to hear the word of God, he saw two boats there at the shore of the lake; the fishermen had gone out of them and were washing their nets. He got into one of the boats, the one belonging to Simon, and asked him to put out a little way from the shore. Then he sat down and taught the crowds from the boat. When he had finished speaking, he said to Simon, "Put out into the deep water and let down your nets for a catch." Simon answered, "Master, we have worked all night long but have caught nothing. Yet if you say so, I will let down the nets." When they had done this, they caught so many fish that their nets were beginning to break. So they signaled their partners in the other boat to come and help them. And they came and filled both boats, so that they began to sink. But when Simon Peter saw it, he fell down at Jesus' knees, saying, "Go away from me, Lord, for I am a sinful man!" For he and all who were with him were amazed at the catch of fish that they had taken; and so also were James and John, sons of Zebedee, who were partners with Simon. Then Jesus said to Simon, "Do not be afraid; from now on you will be catching people." When they had brought their boats to shore, they left everything and followed him.

1. What might have been the shrunken gospel that Simon Peter was living with?

2. What evidence is there in this story that Jesus is inviting the first disciples into a magnificent story?

3. If you were in this story, who would you be (a bystander, a fellow fisherman, maybe Simon Peter)? Why do you see yourself in that place?

4. Has there been a time you have felt Jesus' call to drop the net of your old, shrunken story and join God in some type of adventure? How did it go? How were you changed by it?

Reflecting

This week your soul training exercise focused on goodness.

1. What acts of goodness did you see?

2. Where did you witness ugliness (goodness turned upside down)? How did it affect you?

3. What did you learn about God, yourself, and others from this exercise?

Closing

End your time together by reading aloud the following quote:

We need a story that makes us quiver, not with fear but with delight. We need a story so big that we will never be able to grasp it, so vast that it can handle the darkness of evil and suffering, so immense that it can make sense of cancer and terrorism.

May we continue searching for this magnificent story!

CHAPTER 3: PARTICIPATING IN THE TRINITY

Gathering

If possible, print or project the image of Rublev's Trinity icon. (It can easily be found online.) Begin your time together discussing this depiction of the Trinity. Spend a few minutes looking at the image's details and connecting the significance of those elements as described by the author. What in this icon speaks to you? What have you been taught previously about the Trinity? How has your understanding of the Trinity affected your relationship to the Lord?

Exploring

1. Genesis 1:26 says, "Then God said, 'Let us make humankind in our image, according to our likeness.'" Have you ever noticed the word *us* in this passage? How would you explain the presence of that word?

2. The author summarizes the two false narratives this way: "There is no need for the Trinity" and "Jesus is the asbestos suit that saves us from the white-hot wrath of God." Which has been more common in your journey? How has it affected you? Do you agree with the author that neither of the false narratives are beautiful or good? Why?

3. Spend a few minutes discussing and clarifying your understanding of John Wesley's Quadrilateral. What questions do you have about this model? What would you add to this model?

1. The author describes the nature of the Trinity with the words *kenosis* and *perichoresis* (pp. 46-49). Review his explanation of these terms. How does this imagery change your understanding of God? How does the image of the Trinity joyfully dancing make you feel?

2. The author points out that trinitarian teaching can bring awe, wonder, and joy into our spiritual journey. How does the hope of awe, wonder, and joy draw you into the magnificent story of the Trinity?

Engaging

The author quotes several Scripture passages that speak of the Trinity, including Matthew 3:16-17 and Galatians 4:6. Read aloud this passage from Galatians 4:1-7:

> My point is this: heirs, as long as they are minors, are no better than slaves, though they are the owners of all the property; but they remain under guardians and trustees until the date set by the father. So with us; while we were minors, we were enslaved to the elemental spirits of the world. But when the fullness of time had come, God sent his Son, born of a woman, born under the law, in order to redeem those who were under the law, so that we might receive adoption as children. And because you are children, God has sent the Spirit of his Son into our hearts, crying, "Abba! Father!" So you are no longer a slave but a child, and if a child then also an heir, through God.

1. What does this passage teach you about the nature of the Trinity?

2. How does this Scripture draw you into God's magnificent story?

3. What does it mean to you to be a child and "an heir through God"?

4. What questions about the Trinity remain unanswered for you?

Reflecting

This week your soul training exercise focused on truth.

1. What did you notice as you observed truth in the world?

2. Did you see people behaving and speaking in truth?

3. Did you see truth in surprising ways?

4. How did observing truth affect your understanding of God?

Bonus Practice

1. Did you try the bonus practice of making the sign of the cross? If so, were you able to be mindful of the symbolism of this gesture?

2. How did it affect you?

3. Why might we be cautious in practicing this gesture?

Closing

End your time together with this quote from John O'Donohue:

The Christian concept of god as Trinity is the most sublime articulation of otherness and intimacy, an eternal interflow of friendship. This perspective discloses the beautiful fulfillment of our immortal longing in the words of Jesus, who said, Behold, I call you friends. Jesus, as the son of God, is the first Other in the universe. . . . In friendship with him, we enter the tender beauty and affection of the Trinity. In the embrace of this eternal friendship, we dare to be free.

May we experience the embrace of the eternal friendship, and dare to live in that freedom!

CHAPTER 4: BATHING IN BEAUTY

Gathering

The author shares this description of a moment of experiencing God's love through beauty:

> As I write, I am watching Nebraska's North Loup River gently flow and sparkle as it reflects the sunlight. My dog, Winston, is sleeping at my feet. I am listening to music by the brilliant composer Ludovico Einaudi. Wild turkeys will be coming by to roost in the trees to the south of the cabin. Across the river the cows and their calves are anxiously mooing; this morning the farmer separated them for weaning. There is a pulsing energy around me I used to fail to see. Now I am moved to doxology, to praise God. A rhythm is going on around me. Like Simone Weil, I am learning to see Jesus' "tender smile for us coming through matter."

Individually, recall a time you had eyes to see Jesus' "tender smile for [you] coming through matter." Then as a group discuss what that time was like. What did you notice? What was your doxology in that moment?

Exploring

1. The author articulates this false narrative: "Beauty has nothing to do with God or the Christian life—and it may lead us away from God." What have you been taught (or not taught) about beauty and the Christian life?

2. In your own words, describe the way beauty serves as the *penultimate*, leading to God, who is the ultimate.

3. In the "Tradition" section, the author cites Christian theologians and thinkers from St. Augustine to Hans Urs von Balthasar. As you look over this section, which quote or description do you find most inspiring or helpful?

4. Consider this quote from Balthasar: "Everything that is—every tree, bird, star, stone and wave—existed first as a dream in the mind of the divine artist. Indeed, the world is the mirror of the divine imagination and to decipher the depths of the world is to gain deep insights into the heart of God." How does that make you feel?

5. The author explains that *util* means "useful, beneficial, helpful," and *frui* means "enjoyable, pleasurable, and delightful." He points out that the created world is both *frui* and *util* at the same time. This blend of benefit and delight reveals a God who not only wants us to survive but to thrive. How does this proclamation change your understanding of God and the beauty of the world around you?

Engaging

The true narrative of this chapter is that beauty is a portal to God. And, as the author pointed out, Scripture rarely refers to beauty but does speak of the *glory* of God, which is goodness, beauty, and truth with power. With this in mind, read aloud the following passage from Psalm 19, and discuss the questions below.

> The heavens are telling the glory of God;
>   and the firmament proclaims his handiwork.
> Day to day pours forth speech,
>   and night to night declares knowledge.
> There is no speech, nor are there words;
>   their voice is not heard;
> yet their voice goes out through all the earth,
>   and their words to the end of the world. (Psalm 19:1-4)

1. Take a few minutes and rewrite this psalm in your own words. Consider what the psalmist is saying about God's goodness, beauty, and truth through creation. If you are comfortable, share what you have written with the group.

2. How does this Scripture draw you into God's magnificent story?

3. How could you honor this Scripture in your daily life?

Reflecting

This week your soul training exercise used sight to observe beauty and be drawn closer to God.

1. Where did you spend time looking at beauty?

2. What was your response to the beauty you saw (awe, silence, tears)?

3. How did the thing of beauty draw you toward God? What might it teach you about God?

Closing

End your time together with this quote from Brian Zahnd:

> Our task is not to protest the world into a certain moral conformity, but to attract the world to the saving beauty of Christ.

Let us embrace this task with joy, awe, and wonder!

CHAPTER 5: EMBRACING OUR GOODNESS

Gathering

Begin your time together by listening to a recording of "Hold Me Jesus" by Rich Mullins. If you want to hear Rich being vulnerable about his struggle with temptation and how it led to the writing of this song, you can hear him tell the story on this YouTube clip: "Beaker Wouldn't Snore (Hold Me Jesus)," www.youtube.com /watch?v=6csWlQ9dfb4.

What surprises you about the author's opening story of his conversation with Rich Mullins? How might you have responded to Mullins? Does it challenge your understanding of Christianity to see God doing amazing things through broken, sinful people?

Exploring

1. The dominant narrative of the shaming story is that we are sinful by nature (to the core). In what ways have you been exposed to this narrative? How have you grappled with it?

2. The truth about our nature is that we are originally good. As the author writes, "The Trinity is beautiful, good, and true. We are made in God's image. . . . This means that we are—in our essence—beautiful, good, and true." How does that make you feel?

3. In your own experience, can you see how temptations are distortions of truth, goodness, and beauty? And do those temptations make the penultimate into the ultimate?

4. The good news of this chapter is that we don't need to hide. The author recalls the wisdom in Rich Mullins's confession and transparency. Has there ever been a person or group of people you were able to be honest with and name your struggles? How did that vulnerability change you?

Engaging

This chapter takes us back to Galatians 4, but now we are adding verses 8-10. Read the passage aloud:

> My point is this: heirs, as long as they are minors, are no better than slaves, though they are the owners of all the property; but they remain under guardians and trustees until

the date set by the father. So with us; while we were minors, we were enslaved to the elemental spirits of the world. But when the fullness of time had come, God sent his Son, born of a woman, born under the law, in order to redeem those who were under the law, so that we might receive adoption as children. And because you are children, God has sent the Spirit of his Son into our hearts, crying, "Abba! Father!" So you are no longer a slave but a child, and if a child then also an heir, through God.

Formerly, when you did not know God, you were enslaved to beings that by nature are not gods. Now, however, that you have come to know God, or rather to be known by God, how can you turn back again to the weak and beggarly elemental spirits? How can you want to be enslaved to them again? You are observing special days, and months, and seasons, and years.

1. In light of verses 1 through 8, what does it mean to you to be known by God?

2. According to this passage, what would you say are Paul's words for the shaming story? The magnificent story?

3. How could you apply this teaching to your own life and story?

Reflecting

This week your soul training exercise was utilizing your sense of hearing to observe beauty and be drawn closer to God.

1. What beautiful sounds did you listen to?

2. What was your response to the beauty you heard? How did the act of intentionally listening make you feel?

3. Did God speak to you through the sounds you listened to? If so, what was God telling you?

Closing

End your time together with this quote from Michel Quoist:

> We are not God. We are simply the image of God and our
> task is gradually to discover that image and set it free.

May we embrace this task in all we do!

CHAPTER 6: DISCOVERING THE TRUTH

Gathering

The author begins this chapter with the theological conversation about Jesus from *Talladega Nights*. Drawing from that conversation, the author says, "Like Ricky Bobby, we can choose which Jesus we like: baby Jesus, teacher Jesus, or savior Jesus. But Jesus cannot be reduced to any one of them." What aspects of Jesus' identity are you most comfortable with? What characteristics of Jesus make you the most uncomfortable? Discuss why this is so.

Exploring

1. Discuss this quote from C. S. Lewis: "The Christian story is precisely the story of one grand miracle, the Christian assertion being that what is beyond all space and time, which is uncreated, eternal, came into Nature, into human nature, descended into His own universe, and rose again, bringing Nature up with Him. It is precisely one great miracle." What does Lewis mean by the phrase "one grand miracle"? How does this idea affect your understanding of the Christian story?

2. In explaining the incarnation, the author writes, "The incarnation is a statement of unconditional love. In the incarnation we experience the solidarity of God with humanity." Take a few minutes to write down in your own words why the incarnation is a statement of unconditional love. After

you've written your answer, discuss your explanations with your group.

3. On page 98, the author describes how Jesus did all he did "so we could live in communion with God. In other words, so we could experience eternal life. Now." In what ways does it challenge you to think of eternal life beginning now? And what does this understanding of eternal life mean for you—now?

4. The author points out that Jesus and his love are *knowable*. Can you recall a time you have *known* the love of Jesus? If you are willing, please share your experience with the group. How might you express "wow" and "thanks" to the Lord for his love?

Engaging

The image of the invisible God:

> He is the image of the invisible God, the firstborn of all creation; for in him all things in heaven and on earth were created, things visible and invisible, whether thrones or dominions or rulers or powers—all things have been created through him and for him. He himself is before all things, and in him all things hold together. He is the head of the body, the church; he is the beginning, the firstborn from the dead, so that he might come to have first place in everything. (Colossians 1:15-18)

The author explains the importance of this Scripture by saying,

> It changes the story entirely. Jesus is not just a great teacher. He's not only a sacrificial lamb. Jesus is the one through whom all things came into being, and without him not one thing came into being. Now, his teaching and his sacrifice take on a whole new meaning. If Jesus were just a man, or even a man

with special powers, he could not "make all things new." He might be wise, he might be able to heal, and he might be able to walk on water, but he cannot redeem the entire world— unless he is the Creator and Sustainer of everything.

1. What word or phrase from this passage speaks most power-fully to you? How might you keep that word or phrase before you for a season?

2. How is the redemption story of Christianity transformed when we see Christ as the Creator and Sustainer of every-thing?

3. Reflect on your day. As you go through the different aspects of your day, picture Jesus as the Creator and Sustainer of all the goodness, beauty, and truth you experience. How does this perspective change the way you look at the world?

Reflecting

This week your soul training exercise used your sense of smell to observe beauty and be drawn closer to God.

1. What were a few of the beautiful smells that caught your at-tention? What memories and feelings did those smells evoke for you?

2. How did these smells affect your relationship with God?

3. In what ways could you continue being attentive to smells and allowing them to point you toward God?

Closing

Close with this prayer of proclamation by Bernard of Clairvaux:

How beautiful you appear to the angels, Lord Jesus, in the form of God, eternal, begotten before the daystar amid the splendours of heaven, "the radiant light of God's glory and the perfect copy of his nature," the unchanging and untarnished brightness of eternal life? How beautiful you are to me, my Lord, even in the very discarding of your beauty!

Amen!

CHAPTER 7: GOING THE DISTANCE

Gathering

The author opens this chapter with the devastating information that his daughter Madeline might not live. What is your reaction to this story? What emotions did it stir within you?

Exploring

1. Read these sentences aloud: "Salvation is more than getting into heaven after death. It's freedom from the enemies that destroy us: the law, which creates sin, which creates death. We face two other enemies: suffering and abandonment." How does this powerful understanding of salvation change the way we live?

2. The author lists several metaphors to understand the atonement accomplished on the cross: ransom, reconciliation, satisfaction, appeal of love, and substitution. Which of these metaphors are you most familiar and comfortable with? Which one are you least comfortable with? Why?

3. The author explains that through the descent of Holy Saturday, Jesus experienced abandonment. He writes, "Only trinitarian theology can help us begin to grapple with the idea of God being abandoned by God, but that is what Saturday is all about." What have you been taught previously about Holy Saturday? How does this explanation change your understanding and feeling about Holy Week?

4. In personally connecting Jesus' experience of suffering and abandonment, the author writes, "God is not a cosmic sadist who inflicts suffering on humans. He is a loving Savior who willingly enters into our suffering. I felt abandoned by God when we learned about our daughter's condition. Jesus felt and experienced a far worse abandonment. I felt alone and suffered in silence on many days. But Jesus, I now know, was with me all the time—in complete solidarity. He experienced it with and for me." Take a few minutes to reflect on a time you have felt abandoned by God. Can you picture Jesus standing with you in solidarity? How does such solidarity change our relationship to suffering and to God?

Engaging

Begin by reading Philippians 2:5-11 aloud.

Let the same mind be in you that was in Christ Jesus,

who, though he was in the form of God,
   did not regard equality with God
   as something to be exploited,
but emptied himself,
   taking the form of a slave,
   being born in human likeness.
And being found in human form,
   he humbled himself
   and became obedient to the point of death—
   even death on a cross.

Therefore God also highly exalted him
   and gave him the name
   that is above every name,
so that at the name of Jesus

every knee should bend,
in heaven and on earth and under the earth,
and every tongue should confess
that Jesus Christ is Lord,
to the glory of God the Father.

1. Reread verse 5 through the first three lines of verse 7. These verses connect back to chapter six and our discussion of the significance of the incarnation. Briefly share what you remember about the importance of the incarnation.

2. Read aloud the last line of verses 7-8. Of this movement, the author writes that Jesus is called to "to experience the worst that humans are capable of (and that humans can experience). In so doing, the Trinity will rescue us from our enemies." What does it mean to you, that by this journey you are being rescued?

3. Conclude by slowly reading verses 9-11, savoring Jesus Christ as Lord, the Creator and Sustainer of all things. What is one way you can praise Christ and celebrate what he has done for you personally and for all of humanity?

Reflecting

1. As you spent time touching different materials, did you have insights into God's presence with you? Describe that presence.

2. Reflect on your practice of meditating on the Christ-Form in the passage from John 4. What did you notice when you placed yourself in the story?

3. What from the story made you say "wow!"?

4. As you *waited*, what did you feel the Holy Spirit was inviting you to know or do?

Closing

Close with this quote from Isidore of Seville:

> Today he is, as king, come to the prison; today he has broken
> down the doors of bronze and has snapped the bolts of iron.
> He who, a dead man like any other, was swallowed up, and
> has laid Hell waste in God.

Amen!

CHAPTER 8: MAKING ALL THINGS NEW

Gathering

To begin, review the quote from J. R. R. Tolkien's short story "Leaf
by Niggle." From that story, the author observes, "What did Niggle
realize? That his art—the work he did in his life—was a gift. But
even more, he discovers that the work he did in his life would find
its full completion in the life to come." And he concludes by reflecting on how it will feel someday when he and his wife, Meghan,
see their daughter Madeline again. As a group, discuss the works you
have devoted yourselves to and the dreams you have pursued. What
might it feel like to someday see those works completed and whole?

Exploring

1. The author opens this chapter by recounting his experience of
   watching the movie *A Thief in the Night*. Have you seen this
   movie or read any of the Left Behind series? If so, how did
   you respond to it? Discuss your reaction to the author's explanation of the flaws of the rapture theory.

2. How we expect the story to end determines how we live in
   the world. The author writes, "Those who have died and
   risen with Jesus are resurrection people, and as such are
   now partners in redeeming this world, not abandoning it.

Christ-followers are called to be engaged with the renewal of human culture—on earth, as it is in heaven."

3. Have you ever thought of life's pleasures as sacraments that point to something beyond themselves? How does this perspective change the way we live our everyday lives?

Engaging

Take a few minutes to look over the key Scripture passages used to present the idea of the new heavens and the new earth: Matthew 19:28; Acts 3:20-21; 2 Peter 3:13; Revelation 22:1-2.

1. As you look at these Scripture passages, how do they challenge the assumptions of the scary story and the fluffy place story?

2. What do these Scriptures add to the magnificent story?

3. How are you called to live based on these passages?

Reflecting

The soul training exercise was to notice the beauty of food, and possibly do so with a group of friends as you watched *Babette's Feast*.

1. What was difficult about the process of savoring your meal and noticing the beauty of what you were eating?

2. What were the positive results of this practice?

3. Were you able to turn to God with praise as you ate a meal with intentionality? If so, how did that feel for you? If not, what prevented you?

4. If you were able to watch the movie *Babette's Feast*, discuss what in this movie spoke to you.

Closing

End your time with this N. T. Wright quote:

God is not going to abolish the universe of space, time and matter; he is going to renew it, to restore it, to fill it with new joy and purpose and delight, to take from it all that has corrupted it. . . . New creation has begun in Jesus. There is a pilgrim highway leading all the way from the cross and the empty tomb right through to God's new creation.

Let us go forth from this place and walk this pilgrim highway together!

CHAPTER 9: LIVING IN THE MAGNIFICENT WAY

Gathering

The author writes, "[Jesus] is the master Teacher, and we are his apprentices. The magnificent story naturally leads us to be Jesus' apprentices. Unlike the other shrunken stories, the magnificent story is designed for us to enter into it, and thus to have the story *enter* us." Can you think of people you would describe as having entered the magnificent story, and the story has begun to *enter* them? What stands out to you about these people and the Jesus they follow?

Exploring

1. The author opens the chapter by describing the life of his dog, Winston, and how Winston lives with trust, loyalty, freedom, playfulness, and presumption. How are these indicators of living in the magnificent story?

2. In this chapter we learn that the early Christians did not refer to their religion as Christian. Instead, they described themselves as persons on the Way. What would it mean to you to be a person on the Way?

3. Has your experience of Christianity lacked a narrative larger than yourself? How has that affected your faith journey? In

what ways has this book expanded the magnificent story of Christianity for you?

4. The author offers these important clarifications: "Knowledge always precedes faith. When we know something, we can act on it. Knowledge is the ability to re-present something in an appropriate manner." Spend time discussing the fact that knowledge precedes faith. How is this different from the normal understanding of faith? Spend time discussing knowledge, particularly the fact that it is not only mental but also experiential and bodily.

5. The author describes Jesus as the "revolutionary revolutionist" with four marks to his revolutionary movement, which are (1) a unified and coherent vision of the world, history, and reality; (2) a definite goal to work for, live for, and die for; (3) a call to all people for a common fraternity; and (4) a sense of commitment and a mission to spread the good news that there is hope for the hopeless. In your own words, describe the Way of Jesus using these four requirements.

Engaging
Read through John 14:1-7 twice.

"Do not let your hearts be troubled. Believe in God, believe also in me. In my Father's house there are many dwelling places. If it were not so, would I have told you that I go to prepare a place for you? And if I go and prepare a place for you, I will come again and will take you to myself, so that where I am, there you may be also. And you know the way to the place where I am going." Thomas said to him, "Lord, we do not know where you are going. How can we know the way?" Jesus said to him, "I am the way, and the truth, and the life. No one comes to the Father except through me. If you know me, you will know my Father also. From now on you do know him and have seen him."

1. Keeping in mind that knowing is not only mental but also bodily and experiential, how would you explain Jesus' statement, "If you know me, you will know my Father also"?

2. Spend a few minutes meditating on Jesus' words, "I am the way, and the truth, and the life." How might you live more fully in the Way?

3. How does your understanding of this passage change in light of what you have learned about God's magnificent story?

Reflecting

There is no soul training exercise for this chapter; however, it may be beneficial to reflect on the different practices you have engaged in throughout this book. Are there one or two practices you could return to? Is there a community of people who might commit to the same practice so you can offer each other encouragement?

Closing

Allow these words from 2 Peter 1:2 to serve as your blessing:

May grace and peace be yours in abundance in the knowledge of God and of Jesus our Lord.

Amen!

NOTES

CHAPTER 1: LONGING FOR A MAGNIFICENT STORY

8   *Beauty is goodness made manifest to the senses*: Dallas Willard, chapel talk, Westmont College, Santa Barbara, CA, September 12, 2011, www .youtube.com/watch?v=XzzzH9z0SRE.

10   *Reality is what you bump into*: This was a common saying of Dallas Willard.

10   *The story of Christ is simply a true myth*: C. S. Lewis, *Letters of C. S. Lewis* (San Diego: Harvest Books, 2003), 288.

11   *Beauty will not allow herself to be separated and banned from her two sisters*: Hans Urs von Balthasar, *The Glory of the Lord*, vol. 1, *Seeing the Form* (San Francisco: Ignatius Press, 2005).

13   *We are creatures with a mystery in our heart*: Hans Urs von Balthasar, *Prayer* (San Francisco: Ignatius Press, 2012), 22-23.

15   *If the too obvious, too straight branches of Truth and Good are crushed*: Aleksandr Solzhenitsyn, Nobel Lecture in Literature 1970, quoted in Gregory Wolfe, *Beauty Will Save the World* (Wilmington, DE: ISI Books, 2011).

16   *Beauty will save the world*: Fyodor Dostoevsky, *The Idiot* (New York: Bantam Books, 1983), 370.

CHAPTER 2: FALLING FOR SHRUNKEN STORIES

26   *Fred's version of the gospel can be found in church history*: The first time we hear a story similar to Fred's was by a man named Quintus Septimius Florens Tertullianus (AD c. 155–240), commonly known as Tertullian. Tertullian was a prolific writer. The first Christian author to write in Latin, he was influenced by the Roman legal system, so he used a courtroom illustration to describe the saving work of God. We humans were guilty, but Jesus took our beating, and we are forgiven. Tertullian's illustration was not the dominant way of telling the story in the early church, before or after his time, but it did remain as a theory of the atonement in the Christian West (Latin, Catholic, and eventually Protestant). Tertullian's approach was this: "Repent, then believe." It is a gospel message that places what we do, not what God has done, at the center.

The next time we hear the story this way is in the eleventh century, told by a theologian named Anselm of Canterbury. He uses the same metaphor (Jesus as sacrificial victim) as Tertullian, but he was more influential. The Roman Catholic Church in the Middle Ages found this story an apt way to understand the plagues. God must be mad at us, they reasoned. Salvation shifted from earth to heaven, and eventually the church would become its only dispenser. When it started selling tickets (indulgences), Martin Luther rose up and cried foul, and the call for Reformation split the church into (eventually) many factions.

To be clear, Luther, Calvin, and John Wesley neither affirmed nor denied the gospel of Fred, but they did not *change* the story.

30   *Whoever, then, thinks that he understands the Holy Scriptures*: Augustine, *On Christian Doctrine*, bk. 1, chap. 40.

31   *Within the beautiful—the whole person quivers*: Hans Urs von Balthasar, *The Glory of the Lord*, vol. 1, *Seeing the Form* (San Francisco: Ignatius Press, 2005), 247.

CHAPTER 3: PARTICIPATING IN THE TRINITY

38   *The three transcendentals have been compared*: This is how Hans Urs von Balthasar explained the persons of the Trinity in relation to the transcendentals. His massive sixteen-volume systematics follows this pattern.

39   *The Spirit of truth guides Jesus's followers*: Mark McIntosh, "Trinitarian Perspectives on Christian Spirituality," in *The Blackwell Companion to Christian Spirituality*, ed. Arthur Holder (Sussex, UK: Wiley, 2011), 177; italics added.

40   *Trinitarian Deficit Disorder*: I borrowed this phrase from Richard Rohr's *The Divine Dance: The Trinity and Your Transformation* (New Kensington, PA: Whitaker House, 2016).

41   *Christians are, in their practical life*: Karl Rahner, *The Trinity* (New York: Crossroad, 1999), 10-11.

44   *the word* Trinity *is not in the Bible:* It was first used in the third century by Tertullian.

45   *Bishops gathered at church councils*: At the Council of Nicaea they gathered to deal with a false teaching about the nature of Jesus: Was he God or man? Arius, a popular teacher, proclaimed that Jesus was not a preexistent member of the Godhead but was created by the Father and was less than the Father. Jesus, he taught, was divine, but not God. God created Jesus, who is subordinate, and sent him to save the world. While it may seem like this is splitting theological hairs with nothing really at stake, there was much at stake. If Jesus and the Father are not fully united, a door is opened to many problems, one of which is the shaming gospel.

45 *All things that are in the Father are beheld in the Son*: Gregory of Nyssa, *Epistle* 38.8, quoted in T. F. Torrance, *Trinitarian Faith: The Evangelical Theology of the Ancient Catholic Faith* (New York: T&T Clark, 2000), 63.

46 *There is no hierarchy within the Trinity*: Dallas Willard said this repeatedly in lectures.

46 *There is union without loss of individual identity*: Marty Folsom, "What Is Perichoresis?" *Trinity in You* (blog), accessed December 7, 2016, http://trinityinyou.com/welcome-to-trinity-in-you/19-2.

48 *The Christian concept of god as Trinity:* John O'Donohue, *Anam Cara: A Book of Celtic Wisdom* (New York: HarperCollins, 1998), 15.

50 *Simon Chan on the Holy Spirit*: Simon Chan, *Spiritual Theology: A Systematic Study of the Christian Life* (Downers Grove, IL: IVP Academic, 1998), 72.

51 *Shusaku Endo and Japan*: This information comes from the translator's preface to Shusaku Endo, *A Life of Jesus* (New York: Paulist Press, 1978), 4-5.

51 *The greatest dis-ease facing humanity right now*: Rohr, *Divine Dance*, 39.

CHAPTER 4: BATHING IN BEAUTY

56 *We do not want merely to see beauty*: C. S. Lewis, *The Weight of Glory* (New York: HarperCollins, 2001), 42.

58 *The awful think is that beauty is mysterious*: Fyodor Dostoevsky, *The Brothers Karamazov* (New York: Everyman's Library, 1992), 104.

59 *Today art . . . is the religion of the educated classes*: Tom Wolfe, quoted in Patrick Sherry, *Spirit and Beauty* (Norwich, UK: Hymns Ancient & Modern, 2002), 20.

59 *It is the prerogative and charm of beauty to win hearts*: Miguel de Cervantes, *Don Quixote* (New York: HarperCollins, 2003), 237.

59-60 *People skip Genesis 1–2 and Revelation 21–22*: I am indebted to my friend and colleague Keas Keasler for this insight.

60 *The Bible prefers the word* glory: The Semitic mind would not apply the word *beauty* to God. Beauty is often thought of as a feminine trait. This is similar to other languages and cultures. For example, in Brazil, where Portuguese is spoken, the title of my book *The Good and Beautiful God* is *O Maravilhoso e bom Deus* (The Marvelous and Good God).

61 *Genesis 1 as the story of Someone building a home*: Any discussion of God and creation invokes the great modern debate over creationism and evolution. There is a lot of debate about how and when and by whom the created world—earth, the solar system, the galaxies—came to be. Scientific fact and Genesis 1 have been, unfairly, placed in opposition.

Genesis 1 is a brilliant, inspired story about a Creator and creation. The writers of Genesis 1 were not making a claim about when, and in precisely what manner, the world came to be. Bible scholar John H. Walton put it well. Genesis is not offering a "competing claim to the scientific account of human origins. That does not mean the science is right; it only means that the Bible does not offer a competing claim. The Bible's claim is that whatever happened, God did it. He is the one responsible for our human existence and our human identity regardless of the mechanisms or the time period. The Bible does not say clearly how he did it. Consequently, the Bible does not necessarily make a de novo claim for human origins, though it *does* make a claim that God is the ultimate cause of human origins" (John H. Walton, *The Lost World of Adam and Eve* [Downers Grove, IL: IVP Academic, 2015], 77).

The Bible is making this clear claim: whatever and however it happened, God did it. And God did it marvelously. I have intelligent Christian friends who reject evolution and believe in a literal six-day, young earth creation. I have intelligent Christian friends who affirm evolution and who believe God created the universe via a big bang billions of years ago. I refuse to argue about either view. I am living in what we call the twenty-first century, on a small planet that is reliant on a rather insignificant star (the Sun), trying to understand why the universe is so beautiful, good, and true. Whether creationism or evolution is correct, what I am certain of is that the universe was intelligently designed. Genesis 1 tells me a story about who designed it and how, and I find the story compelling. "In the beginning God created . . ." (Genesis 1:1).

62   *If God wanted to remain silent about His existence*: Michael Kendrick, *Your Blueprint for Life* (Nashville: Nelson, 2012), 18-19.

63   *I asked the earth, I asked the sea and the deeps*: Augustine, *Confessions* 10.6.

63   *Only the beautiful is loved*: Augustine, *On Music* 6.13.

63   *And so it is that all things must desire*: Dionysius the Areopagite, "The Divine Names," in *Pseudo-Dionysius: The Complete Works*, Classics of Western Spirituality (Mahwah, NJ: Paulist Press, 1987), 79.

63   *Believe me, you will find more lessons in the woods*: Bernard of Clairvaux, *Epistola* 106, sect. 2; quoted in Edward Churton, *The Early English Church* (London: Pickering, 1873), 324.

64   *I did not have to ask my heart what it wanted*: John of the Cross, *Love Poems from God: Twelve Sacred Voices from the East and West*, ed. Daniel Ladinsky (New York: Penguin Compass, 2002), 314.

64   *The created world is the sign of love*: Simone Weil, *On Science, Necessity and the Love of God*, trans. R. Rees (Oxford: Oxford University Press, 1968), 129.

64   *God created the universe*: Simone Weil, *Waiting on God* (New York: Routledge, 2010), 60.

64   *We see Christ's "tender smile for us coming through matter"*: Weil, *Waiting on God*, 120.

65   *A moment of grace lies in all beauty*: Hans Urs von Balthasar, *Epilogue*, 66.

65   *There's so much beauty around us*: Rich Mullins, "Here in America," in *A Liturgy, a Legacy, & a Ragamuffin Band*, Reunion Records, 1993.

68   *Everything that is—every tree, bird, star, stone and wave*: Balthasar, *Epilogue*, 109.

68   *Glory be to God for dappled things*: Gerard Manley Hopkins, "Pied Beauty," 1877.

68   *He who can no longer pause to wonder and stand rapt*: Albert Einstein, *Living Philosophies* (New York: Simon & Schuster, 1931).

68   *Balthasar said that whoever does not appreciate beauty*: Hans Urs von Balthasar, quoted in Gregory Wolfe, *Beauty Will Save the World* (Wilmington, DE: ISI Books, 2011), 15.

68   *When we lose sight of beauty*: John O'Donohue, *Beauty: The Invisible Embrace* (New York: Harper Perennial, 2005), 6.

69   *If your salvation does not include living with God in beauty*: Dallas Willard, chapel talk, Westmont College, Santa Barbara, CA, September 12, 2011, www.youtube.com/watch?v=XzzzH9z0SRE.

69   *Our task is not to protest the world*: Brian Zahnd, *Beauty Will Save the World* (Lake Mary, FL: Charisma House, 2012), xvii.

CHAPTER 5: EMBRACING OUR GOODNESS

75   *The distinction between* image *and* likeness: I am aware that many scholars do not make this distinction between image and likeness. But many of the early church fathers did. As Dr. Darren J. Torbic explains, "According to the Church Fathers, the terms image and likeness do not mean the exact same thing. . . . As mankind was endowed with the image of God from the first moment of his existence, man can only acquire the likeness of God by degrees. St. John Chrysostom indicates that we become like God to the extent of our human power (*Fathers of the Church. Homilies on Genesis 1-17* by St. John Chrysostom). We resemble him in our gentleness and mildness and in regard to virtue. To expand on this further, the likeness of Christ consists of truth, meekness, righteousness, humility, and love of mankind (*The First-Created Man* by St. Symeon the New Theologian)." (See Darren J. Torbic "The Image and Likeness of God," *St. George Serbian Orthodox Church*, accessed January 31, 2017, www.stgeorgeserbian.us/darren/darren03.htm.)

I find the distinction very helpful, especially in my work in Christian spiritual formation. We are made in God's image, and it is indelible. But we can, and ought, to grow in Christlikeness.

76   *we were made for goodness*: Anthony J. Ciorra, *Beauty: A Path to God* (Mahwah, NJ: Paulist Press, 2013), 20.

77   *A passage often cited concerning our sinful nature*: Romans 5 is often used to support Augustine's doctrine of original sin. In this passage, Paul emphasizes the saving work of Jesus. Instead of seeing his larger aim, many interpreters point to verse 12 to support the doctrine of original sin: "Therefore, just as sin came into the world through one man, and death came through sin, and so death spread to all because all have sinned." The doctrine of original sin states that we are all born with an inborn necessity to sin. That is not what this verse is saying.

Yes, sin came into the world through one man, and, yes, death came through sin. He then says, "death spread to all *because all have* sinned." But Paul doesn't say, "Because Adam had a sinful nature, and he passed it on to all generations through their birth." In fact, neither *our birth nor our nature are mentioned in Romans 5!* Jesse Morrell states it clearly: "Adam provided the opportunity for our damnation by opening the eyes of mankind to good and evil, but our damnation requires our own choice to do what we know to be wrong" (Jesse Morrell, "Appendix 2: Original Sin Proof Texts Explained," in *Does Man Inherit a Sinful Nature?* [Lindale, TX: Biblical Truth Resources, 2013], 4.7.d). After the fall, everyone is born knowing good and evil. We know what is good, and we also know what is evil. And the choice to do either is ours. Sin goes against life. This is what Adam passed to us.

Additionally, if the sin of one man, Adam, imputed sinfulness to all, then the obedience of Jesus must also impute righteousness to all. This would lead to the doctrine of universalism, which teaches that all people will be saved. Romans 5 does not teach that all people are righteous because of what Jesus did. We become righteous individually, again by choice, by putting our confidence in Jesus. Paul is saying here that spiritual death spread to all people *because of their own sin*. Once Romans 5:12 is correctly understood, its teaching matches with the rest of Scripture: we are all responsible for our own sin. Guilt is not inherited from Adam but a choice to sin is—with our eyes wide open. Because we are human and imperfect, in a sense everyone repeats the sin of Adam.

77   *speech in character*: Luke Timothy Johnson, *Reading Romans* (Macon, GA: Smyth & Helwys, 2001), 115.

78   *Prior to Augustine, however, no such consensus existed*: Karl Giberson, *Saving the Original Sinner: How Christians Have Used the Bible's First Man to Oppress, Inspire, and Make Sense of the World* (Boston: Beacon Press, 2015), 29.

78 *God made Himself man, that man might become God*: Athanasius, *On the Incarnation* 54.3.

79 *There are no* ordinary *people*: C. S. Lewis, *The Weight of Glory* (New York: HarperCollins, 2001), 40.

80 *Michael Polanyi's observation on doubt and trust*: Michael Polanyi, quoted in Curt Thompson, *The Soul of Shame* (Downers Grove, IL: InterVarsity Press, 2015), 101.

80 *We are invariably made for faith*: Thompson, *Soul of Shame*, 101.

81 *In deciding to eat the forbidden fruit*: Ray Anderson, *Theological Foundations for Ministry* (Edinburgh: T&T Clark, 2000), 12.

81 *empty, powerless, dependent, contingent beings*: Luke Timothy Johnson, *Faith's Freedom* (Minneapolis: Fortress Press, 1990), 61-62.

84-85 *We are not God. We are simply the image of God*: Michel Quoist, quoted in Ciorra, *Beauty*, 51.

CHAPTER 6: DISCOVERING THE TRUTH

89 *Sometimes we discover theologians in unexpected places*: *Talladega Nights: The Ballad of Ricky Bobby*, directed by Adam McKay (Culver City, CA: Sony Pictures, 2006).

92 *The Christian story is precisely the story of one grand miracle*: C. S. Lewis, *The Grand Miracle* (New York: Random House, 1988), 55.

93 *Andrew Peterson captures the reality of the birth*: Andrew Peterson, "Labor of Love," in *Behold the Lamb of God*, Fervent Records, 2004.

93 *Chris Rice sings of the wonder*: Chris Rice, "Welcome to Our World" in *Deep Enough to Dream*, Rocketown Records, 1997.

94 *bringing Nature up with Him*: Lewis, *Grand Miracle*, 55.

94 *How beautiful you appear to the angels, Lord Jesus*: Bernard of Clairvaux, *On the Song of Songs II*, sermon 45.

95 *stories which reveal the fact*: Norval Geldenhuys, *Commentary on the Gospel of Luke*, New International Commentary (Grand Rapids: Eerdmans, 1979), 81.

96 *the most revolutionary revolutionist*: I must give credit to my friend and colleague Keas Keasler for this phrase.

99 *It is not our movement toward God, but God's movement to us*: Hans Urs von Balthasar, quoted in Anthony J. Ciorra, *Beauty: A Path to God* (Mahwah, NJ: Paulist Press, 2013), 83.

102 *The central question of the gospel is not how can I be saved*: Scot McKnight, lecture notes taken by the author.

102   *Every human person is predisposed to discover the truth*: Mark McIntosh, *Mystical Theology* (Oxford: Blackwell, 1998), 102.

103   *Jesus is the resolution to a story in search of a completion*: N. T. Wright, lecture notes taken by the author.

105   *It is acutely embarrassing to hear and see*: Kenneth E. Bailey, *Jesus Through Middle Eastern Eyes* (Downers Grove, IL: IVP Academic, 2008), 223.

105   *An enormous amount of sophisticated spiritual formation is taking place*: ibid., 225.

105   *Over time I have become obsessed*: Brian Zahnd, *Beauty Will Save the World* (Lake Mary, FL: Charisma House, 2012), 38.

106   *If anyone could prove to me that Christ is outside the truth*: Fyodor Dostoevsky, "To Mme. N. D. Fonvisin," in *Letters of Fyodor Mikhailovich Dostoevsky to His Family and Friends*, trans. Ethel Colburn Mayne (1914; repr., Whitefish, MT: Kessinger, 2006), 71.

CHAPTER 7: GOING THE DISTANCE

112   *My sin, oh, the bliss of this glorious thought*: Horatio G. Spafford, "It Is Well with My Soul," 1873.

112   *N. T. Wright's analogy*: N.T. Wright, *Simply Good News* (New York: HarperCollins, 2015), 66-69.

116   *One of our main problems about the way the gospel is presented*: Dallas Willard, "The Nature of God's Kingdom: A Reign of Grace," a talk given in San Francisco, 2005.

117   *What did the descent into hell on Saturday actually mean?*: J. Warren Smith and Philip Clayton, quoted in Heather Hahn, "Did Jesus Descend into Hell or to the Dead?," United Methodist News, April 22, 2011, www.umc.org/news-and-media/did-jesus-descend-into-hell-or-to-the-dead.

120   *The early church fathers affirmed the descent on Holy Saturday*: The quotes from Irenaeus, Gregory the Great, and Isidore of Seville are from Hans Urs von Balthasar, *Mysterium Paschale* (San Francisco: Ignatius Press, 1990), 167, 175-76.

121   *the utmost pitch of obedience*: Balthasar, *Mysterium Paschale*, 174.

121   *If it is left out, much of the benefit of Christ's death will be lost*: John Calvin, *Institutes of the Christian Religion* 1.2.16.8.

121   *Then came the march past the victims*: Elie Wiesel, *Night* (New York: Hill & Wang, 2006), 64-65.

122   *For the glory of God is most fully revealed in the descent of the Son*: Anne Murphy, "Hans Urs von Balthasar" in "Theological Trends: Contemporary Theologies of the Cross, I," *The Way* 28, no. 2 (April 1988): 150-51.

122-23 *God "accepted our foreknown abuse of freedom"*: Aidan Nichols, introduction to Balthasar, *Mysterium Paschale*, 7.

125 *Beauty will save the world*: Fyodor Dostoevsky, *The Idiot* (New York: Bantam Books, 1983), 370.

125 *Every cross adorning a church is in itself a sermon*: Brian Zahnd, *Beauty Will Save the World* (Lake Mary, FL: Charisma House, 2012), 60.

125 *We have been created and redeemed for the eternal ecstasy*: Thomas Dubay, *The Evidential Power of Beauty* (San Francisco: Ignatius Press, 1999), 275.

125 *The Christian story is not primarily about how God in Jesus*: Simon Chan, *Spiritual Theology: A Systematic Study of the Christian Life* (Downers Grove, IL: IVP Academic, 1998), 78.

126 *Jesus's resurrection is the beginning of God's new project*: N. T. Wright, *Surprised by Hope* (New York: HarperOne, 2008), 293.

CHAPTER 8: MAKING ALL THINGS NEW

133 *I look on this world as a wrecked vessel*: D. L. Moody, "That Gospel Sermon on the Blessed Hope," in *New Sermons, Addresses and Prayers* (St. Louis: N. D. Thompson, 1877), serm. 16.

133 *It would continue to take hold into the twentieth century*: The history of how Darby's rapture theory came to be the dominant narrative among evangelicals also includes the influence of the Scofield Reference Bible. It was the first study Bible, and it laid out the dispensational theory. Many assumed this theory was biblically supported since it was in a study Bible. In the 1980s Hal Lindsey's book *The Late Great Planet Earth* was highly influential. As a side note, Luther, Calvin, and Wesley would have had no awareness of this theory.

134 *Paul is describing "an escort to earth"*: J. Richard Middleton, *A New Heaven and a New Earth: Reclaiming Biblical Eschatology* (Grand Rapids: Baker Academic, 2014), 234.

136 *God is not going to abolish the universe of space, time and matter*: N. T. Wright, "The Road to New Creation" (sermon, Durham Cathedral, Durham, UK, September 3, 2006).

136 *The church is part of an unfolding story*: Simon Chan, *Spiritual Theology: A Systematic Study of the Christian Life* (Downers Grove, IL: InterVarsity Press, 1998), 113.

137 *definition of* eucatastrophe: "Eucatastrophe," *Oxford Living Dictionaries*, accessed February 20, 2017, http://blog.oxforddictionaries.com/?s =eucatastrophe.

137   *The living God has come with healing and hope in Jesus Christ*: Wright, "Road to New Creation."

137   *the responsible exercise of power on God's behalf*: Middleton, *New Heaven and a New Earth*, 39.

138   *The great hope of Christianity is not that we get to escape*: Keas Keasler, "Honey, We've Shrunk the Gospel," *For the Kingdom* (blog), accessed February 1, 2017, www.keaskeasler.com/2010/05/honey-weve-shrunk-the-gospel.

138   *To focus our expectation in an otherworldly salvation*: Middleton, *New Heaven and a New Earth*, 237.

139   *In the "new heaven and the new earth"*: Hans Urs von Balthasar, *Life Out of Death* (San Francisco: Ignatius Press, 2012), 41-42.

141   *Life's pleasures*: Scot McKnight, *The Heaven Promise* (Colorado Springs: WaterBrook, 2015), 78.

142   *He no longer looked to them like a lion*: C. S. Lewis, *The Last Battle*, Chronicles of Narnia (New York: HarperCollins, 2002), 228.

CHAPTER 9: LIVING IN THE MAGNIFICENT WAY

147   *a disciple is an apprentice of Jesus in Kingdom living*: Dallas Willard said this repeatedly in lectures.

151   *the "vandalism of shalom"*: Cornelius Plantinga, *Not the Way It's Supposed to Be: A Breviary of Sin* (Grand Rapids: Eerdmans, 1996), title of chap. 1.

151   *The aim of God in history is the creation of an all-inclusive*: Dallas Willard, quoted in Richard Foster, *Prayer: Finding the Heart's True Home* (San Francisco: HarperOne, 2002), 254.

APPRENTICE INSTITUTE™

for Christian Spiritual Formation

Under the leadership of James Bryan Smith, The Apprentice Institute (est. 2009), located at Friends University in Wichita, Kansas, provides educational experiences in the area of Christian spirituality, develops resources for individual and church renewal, and engages in research to advance the field of Christian formation.

VISION

The vision of the Apprentice Institute is the renewal of the world and the church through the formation of new people and new communities who have begun living a radical Christian life in conformity to the teachings of Jesus, as his apprentices, in the midst of the world, whether in secular or ministry positions.

PROGRAMS AND EVENTS

The following programs aid in keeping with the Apprentice Institute vision and mission:

- An undergraduate (B.A.) degree in Christian spiritual formation equipping young people to live out their faith as a follower of Jesus no matter their field of study
- A Master of Arts in Christian spiritual formation and leadership designed as a personal growth, academic and professional program (online and residency degree)
- A certificate program, titled Apprentice Experience, is a journey in discipleship intended for anyone wanting to further their study of Christian spiritual formation
- Annual national conference on Christian spiritual formation engaging leaders in the field of Christian spiritual formation

Begin—or extend—your journey of living as an apprentice of Jesus today.

For more information, go to www.apprenticeinstitute.org or email us at info@apprenticeinstitute.org.

FRIENDS
UNIVERSITY

THE
APPRENTICE
SERIES

The Good and Beautiful God
The Good and Beautiful Life
The Good and Beautiful Community

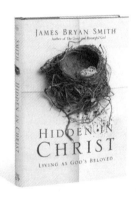

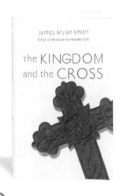

AN
APPRENTICE
RESOURCE

For more information and resources visit
www.apprenticeinstitute.org

COMING SOON FROM JAMES BRYAN SMITH

Fall 2018   Fall 2019

formatio
TRADITION. EXPERIENCE.
TRANSFORMATION.

Formatio books from InterVarsity Press follow the rich tradition of the church in the journey of spiritual formation. These books are not merely about being informed, but about being transformed by Christ and conformed to his image. Formatio stands in InterVarsity Press's evangelical publishing tradition by integrating God's Word with spiritual practice and by prompting readers to move from inward change to outward witness. InterVarsity Press uses the chambered nautilus for Formatio, a symbol of spiritual formation because of its continual spiral journey outward as it moves from its center. We believe that each of us is made with a deep desire to be in God's presence. Formatio books help us to fulfill our deepest desires and to become our true selves in light of God's grace.